MISSING ELEMENT:
The Mystery of ME

THE TECHNOLOGY OF AUTHENTIC PRESENCE

A Guidebook

JERI BURGDORF

S. COLE POWERS
Contributing Author

Missing Element: The Mystery of ME
Book cover image & ME/Missing Element logo
are registered federal trademarks of Missing Element, LLC
THE TECHNOLOGY OF AUTHENTIC PRESENCE™
is a registered federal trademark and Patent Pending

The information contained in this book is intended solely for educational purposes and not for the treatment of any mental or physical health condition or disorder. The content of this book is intended to be used as complementary to healthcare from a licensed healthcare practitioner. The authors of this book are in no way liable for any misuse of the content.

Front Cover Graphic Artist: W. Stacy Vereen
Spine/Back Cover Graphic Design: Chuck Stephens
Front Cover Design Concept: S. Cole Powers

WOOF Publishing

www.MyMissingElement.com

One may have a blazing hearth in one's soul,
and yet no one ever comes to sit by it.
Passers-by see only a wisp of smoke from
the chimney and continue on the way.

Vincent Van Gogh

What Jeri's clients say...

"I always say to artists, managers and anyone else who brings up her name, 'If Jeri Burgdorf had been able to sit down with Hitler for a couple of sessions, it would have changed the course of world events!' " Media Executive, Sony/BMG

"If I paid you every week for the rest of my life, I couldn't pay you enough for what I've gotten in the last two weeks. This is brilliant." CEO, Energy Industry

"The result was stunning. I have never before felt that comfortable preaching nor do I think it has ever been that effective." Minister, FL

"Jeri stole the show...our attendees always ask for more." Public Relations, Hospital Corporation of America

"...unquestionably the highlight of what was determined to be an outstanding day...very alive and capable professional who provided outstanding advice." Executive Staff, United Way

"I think you just explained why my first wife asked for a divorce!" Executive, Dupont, Old Hickory, TN

"It was transformational. A turning point in my career..."

"The potential seems as big as the world itself."

"Revolutionary. Opened new arenas of who I am, windows to my soul."

"This work provides a window on the self."

"It opened up holes in my wall."

"...it is looking at something I already possess and letting that loose."

"I feel that my total being was challenged to be who I am, and to freely express that."

"So helpful in making what I say come alive."

"This training has multiple, far reaching potential."

· Clients' names withheld due to confidentiality ·

—

The authors would like to acknowledge...

~ The "Woofers" for their great hearts and for their help, without which we simply would not have finished this book.

~ Sadhguru Jaggi Vasudev for his Presence.

~ Fran for her courage.

~ Dez Stephens for her tenacious work with the book.

~ Carrie Snider for her meticulous work on this project.

This book is dedicated...

With so much love to my family, especially Peg, Parks, Brian, Cole, Jim and Lena. And to every one of you, here and now, who touch my heart as you travel with me through the pages of *Missing Element*.

Namaste -
Jeri

With love to all my family, especially Jeri. To all the dogs in my life who always love me as I am. And to anyone who has ever felt like something's missing.

Peace -
Cole

CONTENTS

Ancient Ways   8

The Mystery of ME: 10
What's Missing in My Life

A Fear Greater Than Death: 34
Beyond the Limelight Syndrome

Self-Consciousness: 88
Self-Protection or Sabotage

A Disappearing Act: 137
Widening the Target

Presence: 167
The Essential Element

The Magic of ME: 200
The Power of Authentic Presence

References   220

ANCIENT WAYS

It was long before first light when they began arriving – wrapped in flowing garments, moving at the speed of their own nature they came.

First the elders, having made this journey thousands of times, then the children, dancing as they walked along. Wayshowers marked the trail. Firebuilders fanned the flames at the center of the circle, as everyone took their places. Not a sound, as the light reflected off their faces, young and old, female and male.

It was as if the forest began to stir with words – her voice being both soft and strong, "Here and elsewhere we join in this one moment. As always, we are one breath – one stirring – one heartbeat. This circle binds us as we freely join with one another. How could it be otherwise? Never let a new day shine without our sharing all that we are, so that no one is ever outside our circle. No deed, no word, no place, no season can deny us."

The moment filled them, causing some to overflow. For children, it led to slow, rhythmic, silent movements, gracefully floating around the circle – eyes shut – guided by trust, they moved in the darkness. Others, feeling embraced, closed their eyes and breathed in the certain air.

Then, sweetly, another stirring – with a sound like gentle breathing – and the Sage said, "We are grateful for The One Gift that binds and heals. The One Gift known and cherished since before memory began - that we are, by our very essence unbounded, whole and pure. That we are The One Gift."

And the elders began their chanting: "As is…As is…As is…As is…" And the children led the way, glancing toward the circle, backs to the fire, then slowly – freely – with great care they walked the path and turned and twirled and let loose sounds of pure joy – hanging in the air. And, as always, their Lightness invited others to follow.

◊ ◊ ◊

Chapter One

The Mystery of ME:
What's Missing in My Life

◊ What we most want from others...we often hide in ourselves ◊

A small child dances in the aisle...literally bursting with joy...singing her heart's song...twirling 'round and 'round, floating in air...free and fearless. Suddenly a booming voice commands, "Stop that! Can't you act right? People are watching you! You're embarrassing me!" And the child freezes...halts her passion...halts her spontaneity...halts the essence of who she is. And so it begins.

The fear of disclosing who we really are can be relentless. We typically learn it early. For some of us it's a vague discomfort, for others, it's unbearable, so unbearable that we unknowingly teach it, we pass it along. Why? Because even though it's painful to be imprisoned by fear, it's much too frightening to see someone who is not. Because when we're in prison, even a self-imposed one, the last thing we can tolerate is seeing someone who is celebrating their freedom. It sounds harsh, I know. Sometimes it takes very straightforward language to shake us into awareness and out of long-term habits and mindsets.

Two things are crucial to resolve a web of limitations in our lives. Two very simple things. First there's willingness, then there is awareness. With that in mind, read through this series of signals so that you can begin to see how so many seemingly different symptoms can be caused by one problem. Consider which ones sound much too familiar to you. And be assured as you're reading, the solution will follow.

It's...

> feeling like people don't "get me"
> realizing that our personal and business relationships too often go awry
> that incessant gnawing, sometimes screaming in our ears, sometimes whispering in the night telling us we aren't being our best
> thinking we have to act like someone else
> believing we have to be cautious and perfect
> feeling we have to hold back something
> realizing that others don't hear us
> wondering why others don't see us as we do
> seeming to be invisible
> feeling limited and powerless
> knowing that something's missing in our lives

"So," you're wondering, "why would we ever hide ourselves if it's really so uncomfortable, so limiting?"

~ Ironically, we hide ourselves because of discomfort...the uneasiness we too often feel around others – primarily when we're the "focus of attention." ~

And when you think about it, that's a major part of our lives. It could be an interaction as simple as meeting someone new or discussing your idea at a staff meeting. It could be having dinner with your partner's parents for the first time or going out on yet another first date or giving that all important sales pitch to a new client or having that dreaded sex talk with your child or introducing yourself at the PTA meeting or going to your high school reunion or having that must-get job interview or speaking to a large crowd. Any of those can feel as if you're on a stage and in the spotlight! And sometimes it's actually being on stage, a very large stage, as with recording artists whose success *depends* on being the focus of attention.

And it's these very times, for all of us, when we want and need to step forward and shine. But instead, we often vacillate between a few butterflies in our gut and gut-wrenching terror. To whatever extent we feel this discomfort, it is, in reality, fear. And the end result of this fear is that we're stifled, our potential limited. This is a concern of varying degree for every client I've seen, from the superstar to the politician to the CEO to the blue-collar worker.

It's imperative to realize that this pervasive discomfort we have in our interactions with others is very tricky. It can be so scary that we tend to call it something we think less frightening, like "a little apprehensive" or "cautious" or "just a little uneasy." The problem is that whatever else we call it, it's still fear, still there and the focus of our attention, as we relentlessly attempt to avoid it through all manner of controls. But all we're doing is fueling the flames.

~ Ironically, by not recognizing fear for what it is, our attempts at avoiding it only give it more power while diminishing ours as we become invisible. ~

It is primarily within our daily interactions that we either disclose or hide ourselves. And, in our attempts to avoid the fear, we act like something we are not! At one end of the continuum, we might call it being quiet or the classic "introverted" which seems more acceptable than saying "shy." And if that's not tricky enough, there are those at the other end of the continuum who attempt to literally bulldoze right through the fear. They might describe themselves as the funny, entertaining "life of the party" and often say they "tend to be loud." Or they might call it being "assertive" or "taking charge." And then there are those of us somewhere in the middle who might say we're "analytical" or "stoic." It's important to notice which ones sound familiar. We'll come back to it later.

Whether we recognize it for what it is or put other names on it, the labels we place on ourselves are usually about the fear we experience in our interactions with others. These labels can serve as our masks, leading us to believe that we are the mask. Our masks can assure we "lock in" all the parts we play so that we play them in just the right way: the "stern boss," the "sacrificing stoic parent" or the "good daughter or son." All the while we're disappearing from sight; our power is diminishing.

~ Ironically, labeling ourselves is often the same as limiting ourselves, perpetuating the very results we're trying to avoid in the first place. ~

We can try to trick ourselves by saying fear doesn't apply to us. We say we're not afraid, we're just not really interested in doing those things that evoke fear in the first place. Examples might be: going to the strange dinner party with strange people that would be good for business, going out on a first date, accepting a promotion that requires delivering speeches, joining a new bowling team with people you don't know or agreeing to speak at the civic club meeting. In reality, it's because of the fear that we don't do some of those things. And though we try to convince ourselves that we don't care, if fear were out of the picture, it would be a very different picture.

Turning Point

And for most of us, this has become a way of life,
but not a way of fully living.

Then one day arises a choking realization that these self-imposed boundaries have led to missed opportunities and empty relationships, along with the ever increasing feeling of being disconnected and fragmented. A client offered this revelation, "It's the feeling that there's something trapped inside and the shock of knowing that it's me...desperately trying to get out."

Still, we sometimes deny it so that we can pretend it's really all okay. But after a certain point, your awareness won't let it work, and all the while, there's that growing hole in your gut, an emptiness that's no longer filled by a bigger car, a better job or a vacation. In fact, nothing fills it. It is a black hole that now swallows your old tricks.

It's you not getting you, it's you wondering where you went, wondering how the light that is you was eclipsed. And a vague awareness begins to emerge, one that grows with each feeling of being unfulfilled.

Turning Point
What's missing in my life is M.E.!
I am the Missing Element.

What's missing is the real you, the *authentic* you. And that matters to all of us more than you can imagine. It's no wonder that past attempts at "self improvement" fell somewhat short. Why? Because you weren't "there" to be improved! You weren't available to it. You didn't do anything wrong, you just didn't know.

The truth is, you really can't reach your potential in any area of your life if you aren't there in the first place. For that matter, how can we inspire, touch, lead, even love if we aren't really there, if we aren't even available to ourselves? And that hole in your gut begins to feel more like a hole in your soul.

So how is it there are memories of a few times, some distant, some recent, when you actually felt totally at ease around others, even whole and powerful if only for a moment? Can you remember those times? Maybe for example, when you were completely lost in conversation with your best friend, and an hour went by in what seemed like only 10 minutes. Or you made a difficult sale seem effortless by forgetting that it was difficult. Those are the times when you've felt comfortable in your own skin regardless of the circumstance. What a magical feeling that is. You had no fear, and no part of you was looking for the danger. Not yet sure how those fleeting moments of comfort and connection happened, we long for them again. How did I do it before? How can I have it as my way of being when I choose to? There's a great yearning to make the choice for yourself, to no longer allow circumstances to dictate. You want to go back to that freedom, the most basic right we have...boundlessly dancing and singing in the aisles. And it's that awareness, that hunger which drives the search.

Turning Point

There will be a time, if not now soon, when the discomfort of hiding becomes more unbearable than the fear of being visible.

I've had experiences with that discomfort and uneasiness too. I've felt the invisibility, the deep disconnect, the despair and the powerlessness. It was the fear of being the focus that kept me from showing myself, but years ago I discovered that there were also times when I could get free of it even when I was very much the focus of attention. Only years later, when I discovered how to be free of the fear was my life changed forever. So if you will first allow me to give you the details of my journey, then we will work through the answer together.

When I was 12, my family moved into a house across the road from the local radio station. Cedartown, Georgia, was a sweet little town of 10,000 people with a handful of stop lights, phone numbers like 12 and 17 - ours was 22 - and a local picture show. That's what we called it.

The radio station sat on its own little hill and when a good wind came up, all the trash paper and newsprint from its dumpsters came floating over into my yard and the yards of our three neighbors. Most of the paper was Associated Press teletype news stories, weather, features, stock reports, obituary columns, and the not-to-be-missed corn and soybean futures for that day. So, at age 12, I went about picking up this trash from everyone's yard. They thought I was the "good and faithful child" out doing honorable things. Actually had they looked closely, they would have realized that I only gathered up the news copy. I left the livestock reports and the soybean futures right where they fell. Then after my pick-up run, I would hide out in the woods just behind our house and read news copy aloud for hours. Soon I was reading them for Peg, my mom, and she said good things. I felt my natural abilities were good enough because that's what I was told. So I started picturing the radio station's huge glass control room with me seated behind the microphone. I saw the engineer flip the microphone switch and give me a cue, and I began to read in my little 12-year-old voice, "GOOD EVENING. THIS IS JERI BURGDORF WITH THE NEWS."

An amazing thing, as I look back on those days, is that I read clearly with almost perfect control and no mistakes, even as I read the material for the first time. I assumed everyone read this way. No big deal. Another amazing thing was that I wasn't afraid to just be my little pre-teen self as I pictured myself being on the air with no need to pretend I was Walter Cronkite. I was just me. I did this 'clean-up and read' excursion on a daily basis for about a year.

And then it happened! When I was 13, I was

among a few kids who were asked to guest-host a new radio program called "Teen Time." It was a dream! A week later they offered me part-time work as a disc jockey saying, "You're a natural."

But while I was calm and relaxed at my radio station job, I wasn't calm and relaxed anywhere else. My ability to relax socially was nonexistent. Every time I stepped into a social situation, from the after-school corner soda shop gatherings to the annual school prom extravaganza, my senses abandoned me as I disappeared into the background. There was not one shred of "natural" coming from me. I had no idea how to be comfortable in public with my friends, much less with anyone else, and it never occurred to me that I already had the answer, that I already knew how to do this.

I worked at WGAA during the summers through my final year in college, never once being uncomfortable in front of the microphone. People continued to praise my voice and "natural" manner, and I developed confidence. I didn't worry about how to do it or if it was good enough. I just did it. It came to me naturally and without a hint of anxiety. Later, I went into television news as a reporter at WSM in Nashville, Tennessee. It seemed to me there was little difference between a radio microphone and a television microphone. For me, a camera was just another recording device. I was still communicating to a faceless audience. By that time I had developed a certainty about what I could do. My social skills, however, had become an internal running joke. None of my on-camera certainty filtered its way into my personal life. I was so painfully scared, hesitant and uncertain, I practically squeaked. I couldn't do the party or social scene and I couldn't fake it. All attempts got more and more ridiculous, so I just avoided it.

Later, when I started my consultation company, I did so with the idea of teaching clients the professional skill-set that I had developed. And so, I began working with corporate leaders, entertainers, politicians, athletes and other high profile individuals for whom the level of discomfort and the stakes were very high. I began teaching a set of "delivery skills," which to my way of thinking had resulted in my being called a "natural." Clients came to me in hopes of becoming better persuaders, leaders, pastors, listeners, facilitators, singers, negotiators and speakers. And each of them brought a deep need to escape the anxiety generated by situations in which they felt the expectation to be bigger-than-life and smarter, stronger and more powerful than they could ever see themselves being. Of course, it was also expected of them to contain any hint of fear, and so they wouldn't say a word. But they didn't have to. I could see it in their inability to connect as they talked and also in their inability to breathe. That one's hard to miss.

Here's what consistently happened to my clients: Their skills improved in our practice sessions, but when they stepped out into real world situations, the skill improvement was only moderate and they showed a continuing discomfort and lack of confidence. It was disheartening for us both. And so, undaunted, I developed new and better ways of teaching the skills. And the result was worse! How could that be? How could they be less successful as their skills got better? I noticed that in some cases, the better the skills became, the more impersonal the person appeared. It seemed that a very polished set of skills alone somehow translated itself into a plastic and distant person unable to connect with or influence anyone. My clients' comfort levels were also going in the wrong direction.

As hard as I fought it, the light was beginning to dawn that it wasn't about skills and techniques. Something important was missing. The moment I realized that, I found myself with a lot of clients and nothing left to teach. I thought I had been teaching them to be powerful "naturals," but instead I had taught them to be plastic un-naturals. I didn't know enough. It was staggering! I had to let go of what I thought I had known and found myself holding onto nothing at all. I had no answers, only questions. The only thing I knew was what being a natural was not. It wasn't about polished skills. I was stuck. Everything I had been taught and had read was wrong, but what was right? I had so many sleepless nights and day after day of conversations with myself...out loud. But once I discovered what it wasn't, I was onto something. I began to realize that what allowed me to have a comfortable, powerful interaction style wasn't about organizing and preparing or using power words and practicing and memorizing. It wasn't about knowing the other people and *acting* as I thought they expected. It wasn't about dressing just right or the best hair style. It wasn't about a polished, perfect style or delivery. And it wasn't about skills and strategies. What dawned on me was that my being a "natural" was a "being" thing, not a "doing" thing.

It was about being natural, being authentic, being real. But that begged the question, exactly how was I able to be that? It could only happen by creating a freedom from the grip of fear. But how? And I faced yet another set of questions. I realized that what I consistently had in those very public situations that my clients didn't always have was an experience of fearlessness. That was my turning point. On that same day, I made a commitment to discover how I was able to drop that kind of fear. I was dedicated to finding the way past fear that allowed me to open completely to authenticity. And then I had to find a means for sharing it. But I knew that if I could do it, I could teach it. And now, 30 years later, *The Technology of Authentic Presence* is the reflection of that promise.

Writings and theories related to authenticity and presence are abundant, but a technology - a scientifically based mechanism including the "how to" steps has been nonexistent until now. Not only is this technology supported by literally hundreds of "transformation" stories in my work with many thousands of clients, but the mechanisms that support this technology parallel the findings of multiple neurological theories and research studies.

I've worked with over a thousand entertainers, all of whom are constantly scrutinized by the public. This technology allows them to be more at ease and to disclose their own unique qualities, resulting in a powerfully authentic connection being offered to their fans. Think about the superstars. How many are great singers? Some are. Many aren't. But they offer so much more than a perfect instrument. Think about what moves and inspires you. It's not the doing, it's the being. Our connection with others is the conduit that allows the free flow of feelings and passion.

How in the world does our "conduit" get cut off in the first place? How does our most basic right to be authentic get taken away? I think it happens early in life, long before we have the ability or autonomy to choose for ourselves. And it seems to get passed on through families and across generations. Our free, boundless, spontaneous and fearless essence is often blocked. The opposite of authenticity then becomes our way of adapting. Are you able to recall those teachings?

By the way, my social life had a gradual recovery finally. I realized that what allowed me to be fearless professionally could transfer to my being fearless socially. It seemed more difficult, but I was just more scared. It's exactly the same. And I was so very grateful to learn that being authentic can actually set you free.

So our plan is to engage this technology in order to walk together step by step, toward the discovery of that most "essential element" in your life - you. This book is that journey.

In social circles it's called charisma, in business it's referred to as being powerful, in politics it's formidable and in the entertainment industry it's star quality. I call it *authentic presence*. It's your most fundamental right...the right to be who you are.

It is a choice. Shakespeare even spoke of this, "God has given you one face and you make yourself another one."

~ *Ironically, only you can keep yourself from being authentic – no one else can.* ~

Through this very real technology, you will rediscover the mechanism of authenticity. You'll gain awareness of the one way to truly connect and fully engage, first with yourself, so that you will be able to authentically connect with anyone anytime you choose. In that way, this really is a technology of wholeness. You'll rediscover the pure brilliance that is you. And in that process, you will behold the gift that can only be given through this powerful connection.

Turning Point
Our "authentic presence" meets our deepest need.
It is what fills the hole in our soul.

It's a lens by which we can see ourselves, and it binds us to others by sharing the truth of our common ground. It allows for the spontaneous unlimited expression of who we are. And until you are authentically present in your life, you will be the "missing element." Not only that, but the world is denied that which only *you* can bring. The gift of you is that powerful.

~ *Ironically, this isn't about becoming everything you can be, it's about being all that you already are!* ~

It's true that star quality is in each one of us, but it's only available through the power of our authentic presence. It's not about learning long and complex definitions of authenticity, it's about experiencing it. It's not about exploring your authentic presence, it's about living it. It doesn't take months or even days, it can and often does happen in just moments. And it endures.

—

It's not about a right or wrong way to be. It's about having the awareness and recalling the tools you already have for removing the blocks to your authenticity. One of the most poignant moments I can recall came when a client exhaled as if releasing a heavy weight, and with tears in his eyes, whispered, "I've been waiting all my life to hear this." The technology offered here can lift the burden and replace it with freedom while unveiling your magnificence. I do not say that lightly, nor are these words an exaggeration of the truth. It is you who does not yet know.

It's vital to realize that this technology is not about training you, quite the opposite. It's the "untraining" from years of erroneous and damaging beliefs that have served to block you. It presents ideas that will likely contradict much of what you've been taught about yourself and about personal power and fear. But don't worry, being untrained doesn't require years or even months. What it requires is a willingness to step forward and give yourself permission to be fearless. My job is to show you how. Your job is to be willing.

Our goal is not to raise your awareness of fear, but to raise your awareness of the way fear really works. This information is carefully designed to overcome the controlling dynamics of fear, not to scare the wits out of you. You're about to see the plan unfold.

Fear sets off a downward spiral toward a self-fulfilling prophecy by robbing us of any clear vision of who we are. Even though we'll be examining each dynamic within this self-sabotaging spiral in a linear fashion, in reality, this fear ignites an abrupt and simultaneous explosion into self-consciousness, disconnection, absence, acting, misperception and compromised power. It all happens in a split second, with each dynamic perpetuating the other.

But whatever degree of reaction you have to the fear, from a few butterflies to outright terror, these tools will allow you to break that cycle. And, as we move through this material, you'll find more and more that you're stopping fear from igniting the cycle in the first place.

It may sound as if I'm saying, in order to reclaim your authenticity, you have to face the *fear*. Nothing is further from the truth.

Chapter Two

A Fear Greater Than Death:
Beyond the Limelight Syndrome

◊ We are born a perfect Light...only to be eclipsed by fear ◊

So what is this fear about, and what exactly does it have to do with hiding our *authentic presence?* First of all, what I'm about to do is contradict just about everything you've likely been taught about *fear* as it relates to interacting with others. Fear is destructive in every way. In no way is fear helpful. We have been misled by well-meaning people passing along false platitudes.

Consider this. Fear is a totally fabricated "no-thing" which we are taught as a form of control.

Fear is the great destroyer, never helpful, endlessly harmful, the first step in a downward spiral. And yet our global society instills it in the belly of almost every person it touches. It's absurd that we're told a little fear is a good thing. When it comes to being authentic, connected and powerful, it most certainly is not!

See if this sounds familiar. You're standing at the door and you don't know a soul inside. It's just a small social gathering of not more than 15 people. But your body stiffens as you reach for the doorbell. You sweat and switch on your "I'm so cool" act as you try to think of something charming and just as cool to say. The door opens and when you start to introduce your date, you completely blank on her name. And you're thinking how not cool that is, as you ask yourself, "What is *wrong* with me?"

Or you're presenting your sales projections at the monthly staff meeting. You don't even have to stand up, just sit there and spout the numbers to your co-workers and boss. Your numbers are even good this month, so it should be no problem. But as your boss calls your name and all eyes turn to you, your heart pounds, your palms sweat, your hands shake, your legs rattle, your stomach wrenches and your ears ring. There's only a blank where your thoughts used to be. You're stumbling over the figures that you know by heart. You quote the wrong dollar amounts and you're not even aware of it, but everyone else is. And as you look out at their confused faces, you ask yourself, "What have I said?" You have no recall. You lost your place. There's agonizing silence. You're going to be sick. Your mind races, "Maybe I should just cut and run!" And you ask yourself, "What is *wrong* with me?"

Or you're sitting in a group at a first meeting. You don't know anyone, but it's basically informal, just introductions. You'll be going around the circle, saying your name and a little something about yourself. That sounds simple enough. It's almost your turn. The person next to you is talking, but you're not hearing a word they say. You're worrying. And there's that loud buzzing in your ears. And even through all that, you're thinking of just the perfect words to say. You're silently rehearsing your part. Now it's time! Your heart sounds like a snare drum, you turn bright red and look up nervously, barely able to catch your breath as all eyes are bearing down on you, and all you can manage is to stutter your name. Then after an awkward few seconds, the next person begins. And you're *still* not listening. Now you're involved in kicking yourself for screwing up! And you ask yourself, "What is *wrong* with me?"

Or you're driving to meet your father for lunch, and there's a burning dread about what you know is sure to occur. The job and salary questions, it's always the job and salary questions, with particular emphasis on the salary part. "How much are you making now, son? And when is that bonus supposed to kick in? And what about your sales figures last month? Oh, really? Oh well." And you suddenly find yourself thrust back into childhood wondering if you'll ever be able to get your dad's approval. And as you resist the temptation to curl up in the fetal position, you ask yourself, "What is *wrong* with me?"

Or this one, you've just been promoted to department head, and you're having your first staff meeting. In your mind, being a "boss" means being tough, sort of plowing your way right through and proving who's in charge. So that's exactly what you do, as you turn from being basically a nice guy into a loud, inflexible, stern, unfeeling and rather obnoxious character right in front of your staff's eyes. And you leave the meeting wondering, "Why were they staring, like they didn't even recognize me?" And so you ask yourself, "What is wrong with *them*?" And then you're resigned to the real question, "What is wrong with *me*?"

Or you're standing near the center of a packed ballroom at a business cocktail party. And it is truly horrible. You find yourself wishing to be invisible even as you remember that you've worn a bright red gown. You're mumbling into your drink about how sadistic the sponsoring company must be to have a cocktail party of any sort, certainly one this large. And as you make your way to the exit, you realize your effort to hide has worked, and you find yourself wondering why no one even noticed you were there. And you ask yourself, "What is *wrong* with me?"

Turning Point

What's wrong with you is fear.

It's fear that limits you, keeps you disconnected, affects your interactions and manifests itself in people too often "not getting you." Even so, I'm guessing that right now you're still not quite sure if this fear has anything at all to do with you. I promise you it does. It has something to do with all of us. It's just tricky that way.

Fear is defined as "an unpleasant emotion caused by the expectation of pain or danger, whether real or imagined."[1] *FEAR.* To use the word breaks the rules. We're not supposed to be afraid, so when we are, we can't call it by its real name. We use words like reluctant, careful, uneasy, cautious, unsure and anxious. Do you realize just how many times in any given day you feel this way? In our interactions with family, friends, colleagues, the grocery store clerk, the stranger we pass on the street...*we live in hiding.* It's no wonder we feel disconnected, we are.

~ Ironically, while fear leads us to expect the worst, our mentors insist that we should feel protected by it. ~

"But," you ask, "I've always heard that a little anxiety *is* good. It keeps you on your toes, right?"

Wrong! We confuse being on our toes with being anxious or afraid. The only way fear keeps you on your toes is by shooting adrenaline into your system and making you feel hyped and jittery. We've defined it this way for so long, we now believe it.

A colleague told me about meeting a young woman who works at a social services agency. The social worker shared that her agency was shooting a marketing video in a few weeks and her boss mandated that she be in it. Then after a brief silence, she let out an uncomfortable laugh and said, "I already have pre-anxiety about it." Not just anxiety - but *pre*-anxiety! How can feeling discomfort weeks in advance be in the least bit helpful?

Turning Point

Fear related to interactions is likely to make you "edgy" -

but it certainly does not give you an *edge!*

Remember, it's the job of fear to constantly scour

the room and the faces for danger. The result of this relentless search for danger creates even more anxiety and perpetuates the fear, keeping you "on your toes" for sure! Perhaps "on your heels" is a more apt description.

I worked with a wonderful and talented young singer who we'll call Fran. She was from the deep South and carried a "girl next door" charm with a distinctive voice and the kind of gorgeous looks that caused men to walk into telephone poles. I actually saw that happen! Fran wanted more than anything to get a record deal. It was her dream. Her family and entire community back home cheered her on, knowing she could do it. She grew up singing her heart out at church, social gatherings and on the beauty pageant circuit. Later, she sang at local clubs and became the town "wedding singer." She lived and breathed to sing. As she said on more than one occasion, "I just have to sing, in the shower, in the car, wherever. I just have to sing!" Fran had most of what was required to get a record deal. She was the perfect age with good looks, charm and a sultry voice that set her apart from other artists.

But like most adults, Fran also had fear. Her fear was that she might not "perform" well enough when singing in front of others. How ironic that is for someone who aspires to get a recording contract. Actually, it's more common than you might imagine. So Fran focused on being the perfect entertainer, and her fear made her so cautious that she became someone other than Fran. She did this each and every time she auditioned for a record label, the very situation when she most wanted and needed to express her voice and herself fully and powerfully. Fran called her strive for perfection "caution." I call it fear. And it certainly didn't give her an edge.

This dynamic is more the norm than not. I see it everyday with artists, and it's harmful in every single case.

Turning Point

Fear is fear. It masquerades as lesser things,

but whatever you choose to call it, it's still fear.

Think about it. If fear is so awful that we have trouble even calling it by name, how can even a *little* of it be a good thing? It can't.

And how many times have you heard, "Just face the fear and do it anyway?" I think we've all seen how well that one goes. And what about, "You have to work your way through the fear?" Think about that. How logical, helpful or even feasible is it to work through something that's so scary it can shut us down? It's like being in a deep, dark cave with no way out. You can't see your hand in front of your face...so scared it's difficult to catch your breath...the only sound being the pounding of your heart. And you want to spend time there, "working through" the darkness? How about just scrambling out into the daylight as fast as you can! And, trust me, there is a way out. It's a different path. There is light at the end of that dark tunnel.

Focusing on the darkness only keeps you in the dark. It's simply not true that you must "face the fear." Only if you want it to grow should you stare at it.

~ Ironically, focusing on the fear only serves to keep you more fearful! ~

"Okay," you say, "I think I've basically got that, fear's not good, not even being just a little anxious. But you've mentioned 'danger.' What danger? What is this fear really about?"

The "Limelight Syndrome"

You've probably heard of the now famous and disturbing research which places "public speaking" as the number one fear, feared even more than death. So if I might add further perspective based on three decades of experience, I would say that the term "public speaking" represents not just a formal situation like a speech, but any kind of situation, speaking or not, in which we are the *focus of attention*. Although public speaking may be the most frightening example of being on the spot, it's only one of an infinite number.

> *Turning Point*
>
> The fear is not just about speaking,
>
> it's about anything that drags us into the limelight
>
> as the focus of attention.

It's often called "stage fright." But, of course, we're not necessarily talking about a stage, unless the whole world is our stage, made up of an endless array of interactions, including the silent ones.

Our singer, Fran, offered a classic and profound example of this when she described, with total exasperation, how she was able to hit every high note perfectly when she was singing alone in her apartment. But put her in front of one person, any person, and her fear took over.

Does the "limelight syndrome" activate only in large crowds? No. My clients say it just takes one person, depending on who that one is, and depending on the topic and circumstance. There are some situations that are particularly nerve-racking. It could be meeting prospective in-laws, a high level corporate presentation to the board, having your annual performance evaluation, arguing your losing case in court, toasting the guest-of-honor at a dinner, being the guest-of-honor at a dinner, or as with Fran, singing in front of others.

And we might go back and forth, disappointed if the event doesn't happen, all the while dreading the possibility. We do this even with what we consider fun times, like celebrating our birthday with others. Why would we dread something that we really want? Because we would suddenly be thrown into the limelight, that's why. And in this case, it's not because we're the one doing the talking, it's that *all eyes are on us* while everyone sings, "Happy Birthday!" I've learned from my clients that the discomfort can occur on *either* side of the interaction.

Some circumstances seem to hold more jeopardy than others, but it's usually very subjective. A subordinate for example, has more to prove, while his boss has more to lose. An inexperienced label executive is funny as he stumbles introducing an artist, while a senior executive would meet an embarrassed silence under the same circumstances.

There's also just as much variation in comfort level depending on the *number* of people involved. *How many eyes or ears are on us?* Some of my corporate clients are more comfortable in a small group like a staff meeting. But even that varies depending on who's at the meeting and the stakes involved.

In summary, about half my clients feel *less* nervous the *larger* the group. The reason, they say, is because it's less intimate, basically a sea-of-faces. My entertainer clients often fall into that category. The thinking is that a larger audience can't be seen, especially if the house lights are down. Entertainers are looking at the first two rows because they can't see beyond that. It feels like a smaller crowd.

And then there's the fairly unusual person who feels the *most* discomfort with *one* person. That's about the *undivided* attention being on you. But it can also be about discomfort with the level of intimacy in a small group.

For Fran, bigger groups were better. It was the smaller numbers that were her challenge.

Any focus on us, from any person or any number of people, has the potential to throw us off. Different people perceive this danger differently under exactly the same circumstances. But those circumstances always involve being in the limelight.

Our Greatest Fear

What is it we fear about being in the limelight? What sends such a jolt through us that we fear it more than death? See if any of this resonates with you.

It's a fear of...

- Being exposed and unprotected
- Being "found out"
- Being judged and criticized
- Losing control and looking foolish

Why do we fear being exposed just because we're in the limelight? To expose something is to uncover it, leaving it unprotected. Why would we feel unprotected? Why would we feel the need to be protected during interactions in the first place?

Within our interactions, the eyes and ears are on us, and we either reveal or hide ourselves. And, on either side of an interaction, it begins with being afraid that we're being judged and criticized. What do you think about as you look out into their eyes or as you feel them on you while you try to look just about anywhere else?

You wonder, "What are they thinking about me?" "Do I sound okay?"..."What do they think about what I'm saying?"..."Do they believe I know what I'm talking about?"..."Do they remember how I messed up last time?"..."Do I look okay?"..."Can they tell I'm nervous?"..."What if they ask a question and I don't know the answer?" And if we're on the "listening" end, we even wonder if we're doing that right! Have you ever been talking to someone whose eye contact felt more like a stare-down? Have you done that?

Sometimes we do that because we think eye contact shows we're paying attention. When you're doing it out of fear of judgment, nothing could be further from the truth. And there's the classic, "Do they expect me to say something back?" So while they're still talking, we proceed to deliberate, "What's the perfect thing I can say?"

~ Ironically, we fear both exposing and hiding too much of ourselves. ~

SO WHAT ABOUT *ME?*

FROM YOUR LIST OF UNCOMFORTABLE INTERACTIONS, CONSIDER WHICH ARE THE MOST SIGNIFICANT?

- DID YOU FEEL AT ALL VULNERABLE OR JUDGED?
- WHAT MIGHT YOU POSSIBLY HAVE DONE DIFFERENTLY?

Certainly, we've all experienced judgment and criticism from others. And we've all given it. As a society, we seem to do it with as much thought as we give to breathing. So there is a rational basis for our fear, or so it seems. Subsequently, we believe we'll be judged even when it's not the case in reality.

Remember we talked about the definition of fear as an anticipation of pain or danger? Well, this is it.

Judgment and criticism, by their nature, create anticipation of more of the same, and they do their primary job, they instill fear. Not only that, but our judgment is based on some rule we learned in the past about how something "should" be done. We all have them for almost every scenario. And we employ them, not only for self-judgment, but for passing judgment on others, as well. Because those rules live in the past, you have to leave your situation and go to the past to get it, then bring it back. Only then can you can use it to judge yourself or others.

Turning Point
Judgment lives in the past.

"But wait," you're asking, "if I've been judged by a particular person or in a similar situation before, why wouldn't I assume it would happen again with that same person or situation? That's human nature, isn't it?"

You probably would. And you're right, it *is* human nature. Remember, it's the goal of judgment in the first place. And that's exactly the problem. To better understand this, let's look at the opposite scenario. Let's take a time when you've actually had a *good* experience. Perhaps it was a presentation to a small group at work that went really well. You got pats on the back and not a hint of criticism from anyone. Or a dinner party with old friends that was so much fun the time flew by and you actually didn't want it to be over. Or talking with your teenager about a difficult topic and having it go perfectly. Great!

So the next time you experienced these same groups or situations, the next time you presented at a staff meeting or socialized with a group of friends or talked with your teenager about another one of those really hard topics, you weren't the least bit nervous or concerned about how well you'd do, right? I think probably not. Otherwise, being in the limelight wouldn't continue to create fear. And, even if we get compliments from others on a "job well done," we too often don't believe it. Our tendency is to minimize positive feedback and not allow it to carry over in any meaningful way. But as for negative feedback? We keep it forever.

As for Fran, she did have occasions in front of others where she got raves. But that didn't make her any less fearful about not performing perfectly the next time.

And deep down we share this same fear, although each of us believes we're alone in that deep dark cave because we seldom admit the degree to which we're afraid. Trust me, you're not alone in this.

"Controlling" Fear or *Creating* Danger?

This fear can set off a series of protective controllers within us. There are so many variations, but essentially the goal is to duck, take cover and guard the door. We'll talk in some detail about these controls later, but for now it's most important that you allow these questions: If I'm afraid and looking for danger and if I duck, hide and defend to protect against that perceived danger, will I be safe or more at risk? If my controls work well and I'm covered and hidden, am I safe? Can I keep guarding the door? Am I now more afraid or less afraid?

Too many times we create the things that threaten us. It's true. Not always, but too often. First we fear it, and then we think we see it, which then creates it.

And if you expect an attack, what do you do in preparation for that? You will most likely prepare a defense, just in case. So you go into the interaction already being cautious and defended. Now, this is the part that usually runs counter to what we believe: The person who is defended is more likely to be attacked than the person who is not. Defense creates an adversarial relationship under almost all circumstances.

~ Ironically, your expectation of needing a defense will create the feared attack even where it didn't exist. ~

I learned this as a reporter. I would walk in and sit down to do an interview for our evening newscast, and 70% of the time would be faced by an angry person, or so it appeared. I hadn't even asked a question and already they're angry, I thought. And you know what I concluded? They must be hiding something. Why else do they have an attitude? I know now what I didn't understand as a journalist, that these people were afraid and gearing up for the worst. But the result of their fear was to set an adversarial tone which shifted my line-of-questions in an entirely adversarial direction.

Let's look at how this worked with our singer, Fran. Remember her experience in pageants growing up, where she was literally judged on her performing ability. As a child, she got a saturated dose of being judged. And now as an adult, Fran was anticipating the same sort of judgment from others during her singing performances. Even though she and I worked together on "Fran just being Fran," she was too afraid to give up the fear and just be Fran. One of her habits in order to be perfect was to think ahead about coming high notes so that she could hit them perfectly. And so we worked on her belief that jumping ahead in the song to worry about those future notes would help her to sing the notes when she actually got there. Fran was totally open to my teaching, without a hint of defensiveness. She tried so hard. She just laughed when I asked her how she was ever able to hit all the other notes without thinking ahead to those too! But this situation wasn't funny for Fran. She began to get what I was saying, and her awareness of how this process works increased immensely. But to let go of her control was still too scary for her. Here was her thought: "If I can't do it well enough when I'm actively worrying and trying to control it, how do I stand a chance if I stop?" The staggering pressure of her future being on the line allowed fear to rule.

Over the period of a year, Fran sang for all the major record labels in Nashville. It usually went this way: She would practice her songs over and over, get her between-song stories down pat and feel ready. Then she'd go into the label, sit down, wow them with her good looks and charm them with her endearing and funny stories - allowing glimpses of the *real* Fran. Then she'd blow them away with her distinctive powerhouse voice, at least at first. Finally, a switch turned on and Fran's fear would lead her to be cautious and afraid. So fear found the danger, Fran left the building and no one was singing the song. Tragically, Fran had once again created the very thing she feared most.

Fear is a tricky, creative and damaging adversary. We can create a defense and the need for control whether there's a need for it or not. With few exceptions, the apprehension is really not about the particular person or group you're sitting across from, it's an internally generated and self-perpetuating fear.

Turning Point

In other words, this universal fear is generated *within us*.

It's not necessarily about someone else.

Before we go on, after discussing these issues of great concern, I want to assure you that we are building to a solution. In teaching this technology for so many years, I've realized that we must first understand fear in a new way. Only then can we build to the solution.

"Okay, I see how fear is really tricky and a lot of times we create stuff that's not even there," you're thinking, "but what I don't get is about being in control. You have to be in control to do a good job or get what you want, don't you?"

No. The answer is no, at least not in the way you've been thinking of control. This is a tough one, especially for those of us who've been taught the traditional type of control, for example, at the corporate level. But this is key. When it comes to interactions, releasing control is the best way to have it go exactly as you want.

I'm sure the doubt is written all over your face. As I said before, control is a major and very tricky issue, every bit as much as fear. We've all been carefully taught. We all have very finely tuned, carefully honed ways of controlling. Sometimes, especially in fearful situations, it feels as if control is all we have left. It's not surprising we hang on to it for dear life. And so for me to suggest that you give it up just when you're feeling most unprotected?

"You can't be serious!" you say. "Give it up when it really is all I have?"

Yes, I'm serious. And it's not all you have. Stay with me as we unravel the control issue.

SO WHAT ABOUT *ME?*

GO TO YOUR LIST OF UNCOMFORTABLE INTERACTION SCENARIOS.

- WHICH PARTICULAR *ONE* CAUSED YOU THE *MOST* DISCOMFORT?
- DID YOU TRY TO BE EVEN MORE *IN CONTROL*? HOW SO? DID IT HELP?
- DID YOU FEEL MORE PROTECTED?

~ Ironically, we protect our internally generated and self-perpetuating fear. ~

In Our Own Defense

How exactly do we attempt to *protect* ourselves and maintain control when we're the focus of attention and anticipate being judged?

There are two ways. See if they sound familiar.

- *We don't do it. We avoid the interaction.*
- *We do it, but it has to be perfect.*

First, we don't do it. This one is so tempting. In some cases, this is when we try to convince ourselves it's not about fear; it's just that we don't have any interest in doing it. But mostly, we're just avoiding it however we can. How many parties have you missed because "something came up?" How many times have you called in sick rather than give a scheduled presentation? How many times have you avoided volunteering because it felt like putting yourself out there too much? How many promotions or jobs have you turned down because you would have been too high-profile, too public, too much in the limelight? How many times have you slipped around a corner to avoid someone or let the phone ring because the caller was someone you didn't want to face? How many opportunities have you missed? How many people have you lost?

We've all done this. We've all hidden that we do this. We haven't wanted to; we just haven't known what else to do. I once had a senior government executive make me swear that I wouldn't reveal our work together. "Why?" I asked. "Because I'm supposed to already know how to do this," he confessed. Actually, that feeling is more usual than not with my clients. So please know it's not just you.

One major record label executive had a staff meeting every Friday. His role was to sit at a conference table and report on his department's progress in promoting a particular artist's song for the past week. He was the expert. He usually had impressive progress to report as in something to say that would make him look good, like booking an artist on Letterman or Leno for example. But it wasn't about his knowledge or success. Every

Thursday night would bring nausea and insomnia. He wanted to quit his job on Thursdays. He didn't just casually flirt with the idea; he seriously talked with me about walking in and resigning. It literally felt life-threatening to him. He never did quit, but he died a thousand Fridays.

The other option is to do it, but only if you do it perfectly. Remember that our goal is to defend ourselves against the fear of judgment, which may or may not be based in reality. And if we've anticipated that judgment, as we often do, we go into the interaction with a prepared defense. Either way, we typically believe we should do something a certain right way based on the expectations of the person whose judgment we fear. And that may or may not be based in reality, as well. So we access the rule from our past, assuring we'll be clear on the right way! And we believe this particular right way to be *perfection*, in that it'll somehow keep us safe from attack and immune from scrutiny and judgment. This is where the rigidity of caution and perfection come into play as our new "protection."

And you're wondering, "I still don't get what's wrong with doing it perfectly. Isn't that the goal?"

Yes, it is about doing it perfectly, but not in the way you think. When our notion of perfection comes out of fear of judgment, our focus on that fear instantly disconnects us from the interaction and we become cautious and defended. Our attempts at doing something in a certain "right way" to meet expectations, whether preconceived or not, result in *our* being a different way. *Being something other than who we are doesn't deliver perfection.* And whether an expectation is based in reality or not, a preconceived notion can't handle a current situation, no matter how good the plan was. We plan the *perfect* words, even the *perfect* gestures. Sometimes if a client is doing a particularly important presentation, for example, a CEO presenting to the board or a label executive introducing an artist at a label function, they want to carefully get every single word down on paper, sometimes even marking the words they plan to emphasize. And the ministers I coach will spend weeks cautiously crafting their weekly manuscript, sometimes including pre-planned gestures. Each of them is trying to meet what they believe to be the expectations of others. It's not that those techniques are necessarily wrong, but they are unnecessarily limiting.

When you plan based on preconceived notions, you've just put a nice neat little box around not only what you're going to say, but also how you're going to say it. There's little room left for creativity, spontaneity and authentic expression of feelings. How can you fully express passion, enthusiasm, joy or sorrow? How can you *pre-plan* what your future feelings will be about those words? Does that sound like perfection?

~ Ironically, notions of how you should be are limiting because they disallow how you are. ~

If you recall, Fran's fear led her to be cautious trying to be the perfect entertainer. Sadly, the caution and control Fran exerted in order to be the perfect entertainer kept her from being the artist they were seeking - because it kept her from being Fran. You'll begin to see the specific mechanism of how that works as we go along.

Another classic example regards our ministerial clients across the country who often must change churches regularly. Sometimes they are moved from a progressive college town to a rural agricultural area. And what this seems to mean for them is that they have to change. It seems if their congregation changes, they must be different as well in order to meet the expectations of their new parishioners. In other words, to be accepted and approved, they believe they must be an entirely different type of minister, particularly with regard to sermon delivery.

This example allows us to see so clearly, of course, that when a new congregation or any new audience or employer wants someone to morph into something that better fits their comfort zone, they would be asking the impossible. Imagine having to remake yourself every few years, to meet what you believe to be others' expectations. Seem strange? You may do it, or try to do it more than you realize.

At the Root of the Fear

What is it that gives fear the power to make us try to transform ourselves into another person? Even as they tried it, these good-hearted pastors knew it couldn't be done; but they each wanted their new congregation to be pleased, and so they tried to be what they weren't. And it couldn't work because it wasn't real. So they tried harder.

All we can bring is what is real, which is always enough. But if we don't know that, no one else can.

This is an aspect of us that's buried deep down somewhere, often eluding our awareness. In those uncomfortable interactions you noted, why did you feel the need for increasing levels of control?

Turning Point

It's because somewhere deep down,

in a place we don't typically acknowledge,

we fear *how* we are isn't acceptable.

We forget that fear is running us. The standard we set for ourselves is based on our anticipation of judgments from others, but mostly those we've internalized as our own. We forget our abilities. We lose sight of our gifts. We interpret success as failure. You're afraid you'll lose control, mess up and look foolish. So you try even harder to have *more* control over how you're doing.

And even when you do pull it off, you think you've pulled one over on everyone. How many times has that thought gone through your head? Although we sometimes think we're alone in feeling this way - and wonder why we do - the truth is, we're all so accustomed to having this self-doubt that it's become the norm.

But just where did this fear begin? It's curious, indeed.

~ Ironically, where we began was in the total absence of fear. ~

Our opening salvo at birth was as a spontaneous

authentic being, joyous, free and unbounded, totally lacking in fear and self-doubt. A few years later we became the young child joyously dancing in the aisles of the grocery store - where the size of the place, the lights, the smell of the place and the excitement just pushed us over the edge into pure living joy. And we skipped and sang our hearts out, twirling in circles 'round and 'round.

THEN SOMEONE GRABBED OUR ARM AND YELLED, "STOP THAT! COME OVER HERE AND ACT RIGHT!"

For this child, joy and freedom is all they really know. And if someone takes that away, they can't be the only way they know to be. They are frozen. They stop dancing.

"So," you ask, "are you saying we're all born fully knowing who we are?"

It's really not about knowing who we are. It's about being it. We're born being it.

Most of us can recall a time in childhood when we were still boundlessly joyful and spontaneous. And then the day arrives when, seeing as a child sees, the adult in my life tells me that how I'm being is not okay and that I must stop being that. And I learn *fear*. I'm now afraid because I don't have a way to be, and I'm not acceptable being the only way I know. If they take away what I do freely, naturally and spontaneously, I am totally lost. And since I can't make my own choices, I look to my adult for how I should be if not me. So my adult says, "Stop embarrassing me! You're too loud. Why can't you act like Billy?" And there's Billy sitting "perfectly" quiet in the shopping cart. So I conclude that it's not just the actions of dancing and singing that's

—

unacceptable but that *I* am unacceptable and that I must become someone else.

So my memory records two lessons:

I have a fear of being and revealing who I am because I am unacceptable.

So not only do I have to *do* it some other way...

I now believe I have to *be* some other way.

This one instance is just that - one instance. But there are literally thousands of them throughout our childhoods, at home, at school and at church. We're bombarded with others telling us that in order to be accepted, we must fit in, we should check with other people for approval, never embarrass ourselves, not draw attention to ourselves, and be sure to "act right."

Of course, there are practical rules which children must follow. But those are *doing* rules, not *being* rules. Allowing them to be who they naturally are and loving them for it is the primary building block, one that, tragically, is too often missing.

Shakespeare spoke of this tragedy and the vital nature of authenticity, "...this above all, to thine own self be true." Even before Shakespeare's writings, Aristotle's work extensively addressed authenticity in the sense of being true to oneself. He generally viewed an authentic life as one in which a person's individual essence is actualized and their behavior determined by their own values, not those of others.

Turning Point

Early in life our permission to be authentic is damaged.

We learn to meet another's standard of how to be,

and from that – our authenticity is eclipsed.

So we don't, by nature, have a sense of being unacceptable, thus we aren't afraid. But it's the nature of judgment and criticism to instill that fear. From the point of view of the parent or teacher or society, these criticisms are lessons taught with the good intentions of preparing the child for life - to fit in with the norm. But while the intention behind the dynamic is understandable, the result is none-the-less tragic.

As a practical reality, virtually every person learns the same lessons: "Don't cry," "Don't ask so many questions," "Be more like__," "Don't be so__," "Don't show off," "People are watching you," "Act right...act right...act right." And, quite remarkably, we learn that we are unacceptable unless we "act."

All this is compounded on the social front, as we're initiated into our childhood by our peers, who've learned their lessons well and find us unacceptable because we're different from them. Therefore, they conclude something's wrong with us. We see it with various degrees of bullying among kids, teasing each other on the playground and excluding each other from clubs and teams. And adults wonder why children can sometimes be so cruel to each other...they're simply passing on what they've learned from their adults.

In school, we're "protected" by adults teaching us

the "right way" to think about and do things. We're told, "Don't paint the sky yellow, everyone knows it's blue," "Don't color outside the lines" and "Stop talking about an imaginary friend, everybody knows there's no such thing!" We hear, "Don't sing so loud," "You laugh too loud, you're annoying others" and "Stop asking so many questions!" I've heard the story too many times of how, as a child, someone who naturally wrote left-handed was instructed that they would learn to write in the right way, right-handed.

An artist from Alabama told me her school story. She was very bright, probably even beyond her grade, but she didn't know that then. Here's what happened. The class was given a math test full of problems to solve. Our friend, then in elementary school, got almost all the answers correct, but she followed an unorthodox analytical process to get there. And so she got an 'F' on the test. This happened each time she was tested and at the end of the year she failed math. The teacher told her mother that she failed because she got the right answer but in the *wrong* way. That translates to being someone else's ironclad definition of the "right" way. Now, we all know that sometimes life just has to be that way. But the damage is often done unnecessarily. What if that child, in her brilliance, became afraid to explore, to trust her own original thought?

And finally, organized religion can be extremely effective at "fear instruction." From most religions, as children and adults, we hear, "You're wretched, you must fear a vengeful God, follow our rules or you'll go to hell," and other totally fear-based beliefs designed to keep us acting "right." We're told we're unacceptable if we dance, if we divorce, if we go to the wrong church, if we're women, if we're gay, if we wear shorts, or if - in any other way - we somehow are *different.*

Of course, we can learn these lessons by witnessing how others are judged, as well. A colleague very reluctantly went to church as a child, going only to please her aunt. However, she actually began enjoying the sermons as she grew fond of the minister whom she thought to be kind and gentle. Then one day the tragic story spread through her neighborhood that the minister had just committed suicide. She was shocked and confused. It was the first she had ever heard of someone taking their own life. And he was such a nice man. It made no sense. Then she heard that he had been kicked out of the church because someone said he was gay. At that point in my colleague's childhood, she had no clue what "gay" meant, but she learned the lesson that it was death to be different. That was the last time she went to church.

We learn from our well-meaning family, friends, teachers and churches what is unacceptable. And we learn to judge ourselves by their standard.

SO WHAT ABOUT *ME?*

- CAN YOU RECALL EARLY EXPERIENCES OF YOUR FREEDOM BEING RESTRICTED OR OF BEING COMPARED TO SOMEONE ELSE IN A CRITICAL WAY?
- WHAT FEELINGS WERE YOU LEFT WITH?
- WHAT *ULTIMATE* LESSONS DID YOU LEARN ABOUT YOURSELF?

In her fear-driven quest to be the perfect entertainer, Fran was also relentlessly searching for what the record labels wanted so she could morph into that. She even said to me in desperation, "Just tell me who they want me to be and I'll be that!" Fran's fear wasn't really about hitting the high notes and performing perfectly as a singer. It was that she thought being Fran just wouldn't be good enough.

At the *Real* Root of Fear

What is it we're *really* being told? Did those early lessons prepare us for life or did they primarily serve to deny our basic right to live life with freedom, spontaneity, authenticity and fearlessness? Did those lessons block access to our own power by teaching us fear?

~ Ironically, we entered this world as whole and fearless beings. We were authentic and fully connected. We were powerful.
But we seem to have scared the adults! ~

Here is what they really meant. When you were told by your adult, "Don't cry" it meant, "Don't show your feelings." When you heard, "Don't ask so many questions" it meant, "Your curiosity is taking too much of my time." When you were told, "Learn skills girls can use" or "Boys don't play with dolls" it meant, "Be limited to whatever we think you should do depending on your gender." When your adults said, "Don't paint the sky green" and "Don't color outside the lines" it meant, "Don't be unlimited." When they said, "Don't write with your left hand" it meant, "Don't necessarily do what's natural for you." When they said, "Don't talk about imaginary friends" it meant, "You're scaring and embarrassing me." When you were told, "Don't dance in the aisles" it meant, "That's too much unrestricted joy and freedom." When you heard, "You are wretched" it meant, "Don't think of yourself as good and powerful." When your adult told you, "People are watching you so you'd better act right" you were being told, "Be somebody other than who you are." And on and on and on.

Listen to that. What are they actually saying?

They're not really telling us that we're inadequate. They're really telling us that we are potentially far *too* powerful! But they weren't aware they were saying that, and we never heard it that way, and so we learned the wrong lesson.

Turning Point

What we typically learn is that it's unacceptable for us to

fully be and express ourselves.

At a recent seminar, a senior executive in her forties said, "I feel like I'm on a leash. I'm being held back." Another participant said, "This is freedom I never knew existed. It's like a light went on."

SO WHAT ABOUT *ME?*

THINK BACK TO THE EXPERIENCES WHEN YOUR FREEDOM "TO BE" WAS BLOCKED.

- NOW TURN THAT AROUND IN YOUR HEAD. SEE IF IT RESONATES AS TRUTH THAT YOU WERE SIMPLY BEING TOO POWERFUL AND THAT SOMEHOW IT WAS UNACCEPTABLE?

It's important that we unwire and rewire the conclusions we've drawn about ourselves. That is the greatest gift you can give to yourself.

Passing it On

So why in the world do we continue to do this to each other? It's because what has been taught over generations creates its own self-perpetuating legacy. If your parents had chosen to express their authenticity and power, perhaps they could have encouraged you to do that, too. But they were taught just the opposite and passed it on to you. How could they teach you something they didn't know for themselves? This is not about fault. It's about changing the legacy.

A powerfully authentic person, child or adult, can be intimidating to those who are afraid to reveal it in themselves. Have you ever seen someone stare in disbelief and loudly criticize someone who's being completely joyous? Have you ever criticized someone in that way? We all have. It's so commonplace that we don't give it a second thought. If I'm afraid of fully and fearlessly living my life, then I will counsel you to be cautious about feeling, exploring, thriving and being deliciously alive, free and powerful. It's not that I'm trying to harm you; it's that I'm trying to protect you by teaching what I believe to be the norm. In fact, the process of passing this along is so deeply rooted in us that we're usually unaware we're doing it. And we have no idea of its impact.

A business associate proudly described her daughter as, "a chameleon just like I am, she'll be just what anyone wants her to be." I know that this loving parent wants only the best for her daughter. She's simply passing on what she learned.

Turning Point

We weren't silenced because we were inadequate.

We were silenced because our culture wants us

to be the way *it* is, finding anything more than

that unacceptable.

We were silenced because we were *too* powerful

for the comfort of others: too happy, too sad, too silly, too creative, too angry, too truthful, too authentic, too alive, too alive, too alive. It happens because those around us from whom we're learning were taught this way of being too. Your job, in every moment, is to bring full awareness to all that you pass on to another.

We are all teachers. How can we learn to trust our children as they discover and celebrate the authentic being they are in presenting their unique gifts - gifts they *alone* can offer? How can we offer guidance along the way, without demanding they become a certain way, based on our idea of who they should be? How can we invite and encourage full expression of authenticity?

SO WHAT ABOUT *ME?*

- TAKE A MOMENT AND EXAMINE YOUR STANDARD OF THE RIGHT WAY TO BE FOR YOURSELF AND OTHERS.

- DOES YOUR TEACHING AND EXAMPLE INVITE OTHERS' GIFTS TO BE FREELY GIVEN?

I remember the day this happened as an indelible snap shot in my memory. An RCA label executive and I were sitting at lunch in a New York deli. She said, "I'm afraid to open my mouth...that they will see me for what I am." When she spoke those words, I looked into her eyes and just let myself say a series of words I had never heard or thought, "Yes they will see you if you let them, but your fear is not what you think. The real fear is in releasing all that you are - your courage, your wisdom, your true brilliance. The fear is that it feels too much to reveal...too big to acknowledge...and too frightening to show. It's *you*. And you're afraid *not* to hide it."

We sat there in silence for awhile. Then, we left the deli and walked without talking. After a bit, she said, "This is what I've tried to tell my children, but I never knew - " She fell silent again. Several minutes passed, then she concluded, "I never knew it was true for me, too."

Permission to be ME

Does our authenticity require *permission* from others? There's a quote found hand-engraved on the wall at Mother Teresa's Children's Home in Calcutta. It's unknown who wrote: "...in the final analysis, it is between you and God; it was never between you and them anyway."

> *Turning Point*
>
> Your *authentic presence* requires no one's
>
> permission but your own.

Let's rediscover the truth about the power of our authenticity and pass *that* on!

♦ Expressing yourself authentically is powerful.

♦ Connecting with others is powerful.

♦ Being passionate is powerful.

♦ Being spontaneous and alive is powerful.

♦ Creating in your distinctive way is powerful.

♦ Being joyful for no reason at all is powerful.

♦ Unbounded, unconditional love is powerful.

SO WHAT ABOUT *ME?*

- WHICH WORDS ABOVE DESCRIBE HOW YOU ARE WITH OTHERS? AT HOME? AT WORK?
- WHICH DESCRIBE HOW YOU SEE YOURSELF?
- IF YOU WERE THIS WAY WITH OTHERS, WHAT WOULD BE THE BEST AND WORST THAT COULD HAPPEN?

Will you allow yourself to be powerful? *Power* in this case means "to connect with" - to allow meaningful connections with others, to influence, to inspire, to matter.

Permission to be authentic and powerful comes from within each of us. When I've posed this question to clients, "Are you willing to be powerful?" Their answers are revealing: "I don't want to intimidate people," "But then I wouldn't have any excuses," "I don't want to be seen as arrogant" and "But that carries so much responsibility." Are any of these true for you? Are there others?

Our singer, Fran, answered this way, "I'm afraid to let myself out. The only time I've ever done it was when I was a kid and I sang in front of a big double mirror in my bedroom, and only after I'd checked to be sure no one else was in the house, and then closed and locked all the doors. Only then could I stand in front of that mirror and sing from the bottom of my soul. It sounded so different. I've never been able to do it anywhere else. I don't know what happened. I know that what came out was big and overwhelming, almost too much for me. I felt like I couldn't control it, it was so big I think it would scare people. It's too big." On a level that was not yet in her full awareness, Fran's fear describes our own. Our fear is about how much we are, not how little.

Not yet having the insight or recalling the truth, and not yet having reached that *turning point*, we continue down the same path of fear. We stop ourselves by refusing permission to be fearless and powerful. We are afraid to stop being afraid. Yes indeed, we learned our lessons well. And so the fear is passed on.

—

> *Turning Point*
>
> If we look fear squarely in the face,
>
> we disappear into *self-consciousness*.

Chapter Three

Self-Consciousness:
Self-Protection or Sabotage?

◊ To observe oneself through the lens of fear...
is to see only an illusion ◊

When we're *self-conscious* we set up our *observer*. It's a lookout post we use to watch ourselves in interactions. First we're afraid, seeing that we're not acceptable as is. Then we must monitor ourselves to see if the fix is working, an assurance that our performance is going according to plan.

QUESTION: But if the singer is looking on from a distant observation post, who is singing the song?

Our 'Observer'

This is the embodiment of our self-consciousness. It's you watching you through the eyes of fear. On either side of the interaction, it's the means by which you observe how you interact and communicate, as you're doing it. The observer critiques how you're doing. So if you're watching through the monitor, your attention is everywhere except inside the interaction itself. In other words, you're not there.

Once you're focused on fear, you're gone. Pure and simple. You're looking on from that distant outpost and you're disconnected. It's why you feel invisible, because you are.

The lights are on, but nobody's home. Have you ever seen that in someone? It's the classic glazed-over look in someone's eyes, and it leads them to laugh at an inappropriate moment, to repeatedly ask for something to be repeated, to give an answer unrelated to the topic or to just stare off into space. Absence is absence. Either you're there or you're not. You can't be partially there.

When I teach seminars, one exercise I do asks participants to make a mark on a paper each time they "check out" over a 15-second period of silence. There are always two to four marks...in 15 seconds. That's a lot of absence.

SO WHAT ABOUT *ME?*

- RECALL A RECENT INTERACTION WHEN YOU WERE TALKING AND IT BECAME OBVIOUS THAT THE OTHER PERSON "CHECKED OUT?"

- HOW DID YOU KNOW?

We think our *observer* protects us from judgment and criticism.

~ Ironically, in becoming self-conscious, we are our own worst judge and critic. ~

We purposely pass judgment on ourselves before someone else can. We do it all day long during uncomfortable situations. We may observe and judge how we're coming across as we talk, whether it sounds like we know what we're talking about, whether we're talking too fast, gesturing or pacing too much, or making eye contact. And then there's worrying about hair, wrinkles in our slacks, polish on our shoes, and spaghetti in our teeth. And then, if we're the listener, we wonder if that strange look from the person talking means that we just did something weird. And now we're self-conscious, too.

What seems true is that, at any given time, we see a thousand reasons to be self-conscious. But we aren't self-conscious unless we're fearful. So it's not the reasons. It's the *fear.*

~ Ironically, we think that our observer is protection from fear. When, in fact, it is the manifestation of fear. No fear, no observer. ~

Self-consciousness is like quicksand. When we observe ourselves, we lose sight of what's real. We're disconnected from the interaction. Yet, we're literally judging how we think others are judging us. In stereo! And who's the expert on our own worst fears? We are, of course. We know the hidden caverns and deep dark places that are our own insecurities, and we can lose ourselves there.

A client, a corporate trainer in her mid 50's, is readying for a business trip one morning before daylight. As it turns out, she oversleeps, which is particularly alarming to her since she usually gets up much earlier than necessary to allow plenty of time. She's particular about her looks, compulsive about everything being perfect, every hair in place, shirt crisp, suit pressed and, of course, everything color coordinated. So on this certain morning, she scurries around dressing, still half asleep and in the dark so as not to awaken anyone. She hurries to the airport to make her flight just in the nick of time. After landing and running to grab a cab, she finally arrives. And standing before the corporate group, she breathes a sigh of relief, takes a step forward and begins her presentation. It's a familiar talk and it begins smoothly. She's confident. She looks out at the faces, around the room, down at the floor...and she's frozen in that instant...staring at her shoes, one tan and one black! The blood runs to her face. "Oh no," she's silently screaming. "What will they think? I look ridiculous!" The truth is, up until that point, every corporate executive in that room had been engrossed in her talk. That was about to change.

She plunges into self-consciousness. Even though she struggles to recover, it is like quicksand and she will not allow herself to get out. She stands there watching and berating herself through her observer. And in the process, she loses her audience.

Now, you may be thinking this example is a bit extreme, after all, who wouldn't be self-conscious if they wore two different shoes? And you're right, most would. But think about it, if you didn't have fear on some level, would you really be frozen in self-judgment, in fact, would you have *any* level of judgment over the color of your shoes?

I suggested to her that she could have just kicked her shoes off. She didn't care for my suggestion. Months later, it still was not funny.

There are two vital points illustrated here:

First, just because we drift into self-consciousness doesn't mean we have to move in and stay. It's possible to be self-conscious one instant and to recover in the next; in fact, you already do that more than you realize. It's important to remember that shifting your attention off self-consciousness is something you know how to do. You're most often unaware that you're doing it, and always unaware of how. The key is to rediscover "how," which is where all this is leading.

Secondly, when we're self-conscious, we're tuned into the "voice of fear" which is self-judgment coming through our observer. That voice can sound like anything from a stern lecture, all the way to screaming in our ears about how we can't seem to do anything right. Our corporate trainer's voice of fear was obviously the screaming, hypercritical type.

Did your voice of fear give you a little slap on the hand or totally blast you with what an obvious failure you are? The latter can sound like tuning into a doomsday radio station. If you tune in, you might hear, "Run for your life! Fire! Fire!" And this is immediately followed by an account of everything you've ever feared, along with a running critique of the mess you're making of whatever you're doing at the moment. But remember two things: first, you don't have to tune in; and second, if you do tune into your voice of fear, for all practical purposes, you're gone. So you can't trust your take on reality in that moment because you're not even there. Don't trust anything that comes from your focus on fear.

Here's an example of listening to the doomsday self-consciousness machine instead of what's really going on in the room. A colleague was doing a weekend self-improvement seminar along with about 70 other people. She typically felt inadequate talking in front of a group, but at one point managed to conquer it enough to stand and tell a personal experience. Now, you should know that everyone had previously been made aware of the following rule: When referring to yourself, say, "I" not "you" or "we." And the leader promised to correct them if they did otherwise. My friend was so nervous she hadn't heard the rule. So she took a deep breath, began her story and was a few sentences in when the leader stopped her, "You said 'we' when referring to yourself," he said. Then as a way of getting her to see the meaning of that sentence using 'we,' he joked, "Do you think everyone here wants you to be their spokesperson?" Everyone laughed. Well, not everyone. My colleague had been so self-conscious that she hadn't heard herself say "we," nor did she hear him advise her that she said "we." And so she assumed he was making fun of her lack of ability to speak with a crack about "not wanting her to be their spokesperson." Not asking for further clarification, she continued her story in humiliation, the whole time screaming to herself, "See, I knew it, I suck, I shouldn't be here, I'm horrible and I should probably even quit my job because I'm so lame." And she swore to herself that she would never stand up and speak again.

One of the most classic "hypercritical raging self-consciousness" stories comes from a client who was beginning to do professional speaking to small meetings and conventions. During our work together, she demonstrated a compelling talk and delivery. So she scheduled her first engagement and was on her way. She started her speech in a meeting room filled to capacity, feeling nervous at first, but settling into a comfortable pace about five minutes into her presentation. She felt good, felt some energy in the crowd, even got positive responses here and there.

But, then, five minutes later, three people sitting together got to their feet, turned around, and slowly threaded their way between the rows and out of the room. She went straight to being self-conscious, "This isn't good!" she thought in a panic...continuing to wonder what she had done wrong as she went on with her speech. And, then, "Oh no! Another one's leaving!" It was unbelievable. This emptying process continued until half the room had stood, turned away from her and casually walked out. The huge doors slammed with each one. About 50 times those doors slammed! Now she's left with half her group and a ruthless vengeance aimed at herself. "They hate me! I'm a disaster! I'm setting records! I'm so boring I'm running them out of the room!" For another 15 minutes this internal agony continued, as she aggressively attacked herself, speaking all the while. She kept going, but she was red-faced, humiliated, and thought seriously about making a break for the door herself. When the speech was mercifully over, a couple of the remaining audience members came to shake her hand. "Thanks for speaking today," one said. "We're really sorry everyone had to leave early for the funeral." It was audible...her sigh of relief. Everyone in the room had known about the funeral except the speaker. And she had bruised and battered herself without even knowing why. She had been totally lost in her self-consciousness and was completely separated from anything real in the room.

It isn't at all strange, given that extreme circumstance, that she was self-conscious for a moment or two as her audience began to dissolve. Still, the question should be asked, why did she become self-conscious and remain there assuming it was something she did? Why did she judge herself so automatically? Why didn't she stop, smile, and simply ask the audience "Is everything okay?" Now, I know most of us wouldn't do that. We probably would be afraid of the answer. Exactly. Yes it would have been a risk, and it would have been worth it. And it likely couldn't have been any worse than what actually happened.

Self-consciousness is definitely *not* your friend and protector. It's every bit as destructive as its parent - fear.

> *Turning Point*
>
> Fear births self-consciousness, then
>
> self-consciousness perpetuates fear.
>
> And both disconnect us from what's real.

Back to Fran, our singer. After a few sessions with her, she began connecting the dots. She could see how she changed her thinking and her singing on every occasion except when singing at home alone. She began to recognize just how often she became self-conscious and watched herself. And she could see it was *her* preconceived, self-imposed notion of the perfect entertainer that was being demanded. She even realized that any movement away from who she really was as a person might be counter to what the label actually wanted. And she spotted the habit she had launched years ago on stage as a beauty contestant. Give them what you think they want, whether it's you or not. She was beginning to see it.

SO WHAT ABOUT *ME?*

- REMEMBER A TIME WHEN WHAT FRAN WAS CONSIDERING SEEMED LIKE A GOOD IDEA? "Give them what you think they want, whether it's you or not."
- CONSIDER HOW THAT WENT.

To be aware of our willingness to morph into whatever somebody else wants us to be is both shocking and a valuable insight. This awareness of the problem is a large part of the solution.

Step-by-step, we're approaching the beginning of a potential mastery over fear. It took me decades to develop a successful method of teaching this technology. And we are, as you probably realize, handling both entrenched thoughts and beliefs, even as we deal with the fear that arises from questioning those thoughts and beliefs. What you are now walking through is no small thing. Be assured that your courage will be rewarded with a new level of freedom.

The Illusion of Perfection

So part of this process is that we're compelled to watch how we're doing in order to assure it's in line with the perfect way we'd planned to do it. And we think it best to check on our performance by observing it as we perform. Given this, we can conclude that we're planning to be something other than our natural authentic selves; otherwise there would be no need to monitor the "performance." There would be no performance.

So, now, who is it they will see standing there? They will not see a hint of authenticity. And they won't see you, not really. That's the price we pay for self-consciousness. Even the word itself is defined as, "...unnatural in manner from knowing one is being observed by others."[1]   Unnatural.

Remember that this can happen at any level of interaction from a casual one-on-one...to a business meeting...to speaking in front of a large audience. In the case of the latter, people watching you will be used to that from presenters. They've come to expect that the person up front won't really be in the room with them. We're all used to that. It's just that you're treating what should be a connection like it's a stage. And that level of distancing could be perceived as you being cold and aloof, maybe even uncaring. Why would they think that? Because it's not someone else's style they want. It's you. Perfect is not perfect words. Perfect is not perfect delivery. That's your idea of perfection, not theirs.

Perfect is perfectly authentic. Perfectly real. You being you. Don't believe it? Keep reading. You don't know power until you tap into the power of authentic presence in every aspect of your life.

Whichever side of the interaction you're on, talking or listening, the reality is the same. If your attention is somewhere else, wherever that is, you are absent, and everyone will know it. *You can't be partly there.* If you hold back, they're seeing some other version of you. And they won't care that this other version is trying to get it just right.

Turning Point

There is no perfection if you're not in the room.

Is it enough for a great singer to hit the notes perfectly while being emotionally removed from the song? Don't you want to feel the song as your favorite singer sings it? Of course you do. That's not an instrument on the stage. That's a person who is either connected or disconnected from what she's singing. And that matters in how you experience what she sings. We talked earlier about the number of superstars who are stellar singers. Some are, but not many. Why? Because it's not about that. *It's about completely being in the song, about becoming the song.* There aren't many superstars because it takes great courage to be completely involved in what you are singing or saying. No distance. No holding back.

In your world, if you hold back you aren't authentically engaging those you're with. It's as though you're separate and distanced. And, in a sense, it's a self-fulfilling prophecy. The challenge is that you have your good reasons for holding that distance. We all do.

The problem is that those opinions and judgments you're shielding against aren't based on what you think. Credibility isn't built on what you know alone. It is built first on whether they can trust you. Only then will they care how much you know. A colleague in healthcare told me of a related sentiment that says patients don't care what their healthcare provider knows until they know the provider cares.

Throwing your knowledge at me while you disappear into the draperies will accomplish two things:

First, I'll wonder where you went and who you are...that is, if I'm there to wonder.

Secondly, I will not have heard what you said, neither your knowledge nor your message, because first I have to decide that I want to listen to you and only then will I turn up the volume. If you aren't there the volume stays off. Why would I listen? In other words, to put it poetically, it's not the stuff you say.

Do we want to protect ourselves into invisibility, making it impossible to find us, know us, love us? I've done that. Have you? Is that real perfection?

~ Ironically, we sometimes seem to create those things we most fight against. ~

If we're seen as cold or arrogant or disingenuous, we may actually draw the criticism we fear. Not because we're cold, arrogant or disingenuous, but because someone couldn't get to know us well enough to realize that we're not. And if that does happen, then we're likely to become defensive and retreat even further. The result is an insane cycle of misperception and reaction. Suddenly you're under fire, things are out of control, and it feels as though you've been attacked when actually you were the one who painted the target on your chest. And that is why it takes great courage to be the simplest thing - authentic.

So many of my artist clients think the safe way to stardom is by creating an image that won't allow their fans to know who they are. The way I've heard it most is, "I want to be mysterious and I don't want them to know a lot about me." In fact, that translates into, "I'm afraid for them to know me."

What is "star quality" if not allowing fans a sense of who the artist is by sharing the passion that artist feels for what they do? In other words, it's being real. One of our goals for artists is always to have the audience say: "He's the real deal!"

And for our singer Fran, whether in front of a small crowd of friends or a high-stakes audition with a label executive, her self-consciousness led to caution and meant she held back something of herself, in the end, selling herself short.

SO WHAT ABOUT *ME?*

- FROM YOUR LIST OF UNCOMFORTABLE INTERACTIONS, ARE YOU BEGINNING TO SEE PATTERNS?

~ Ironically, our quest for perfection leads us to appear inauthentic, resulting in the likelihood of judgment and criticism. ~

Of course, we all want to be real. We just want to wait until it's safe. That's why it takes courage. We all hunger for the connection that comes from someone who is real whether it's safe or not. *What's true is that being real carries its own safety net.* We'll talk more about that later.

What's perfection for you? What moves you more, polish or passion? Is it what they said or how they leave you feeling? What moves you about people you admire? Is it the great voice or the great heart? Is it the polished speaker or the open approachability? Who is singing the song? Why does "star quality" revolve around passion? What is it that gives leaders and high-profile personalities that special something?

If we know what we want and need from someone else, why is it that we can't find a way to give that? It's just that our indoctrination to the benefits of fear has made it difficult to find *our* way.

The Power of Focus

Where we focus our attention has enormous power. A simple shift makes the difference between being disconnected or not, being absent or not, and essentially, being invisible or not. Let's look at specifically how this works and the part focus plays when "the lights are on, but nobody's home!"

First, when you watch yourself through the eyes of fear, you turn away from the message, both the words and feelings of the interaction, and onto "What's next?"..."What just happened?"..."How am I doing?" Or you may think, "Am I showing that 'executive style' the boss wants?" In other words, whatever you tune into when you're self-conscious, it's neither the message nor your *experience* of the message. You're watching yourself to be sure you're doing it right. If you were more relaxed and without fear, you'd have no need to keep-an-eye on yourself. And if you were without discomfort, you'd be content to be natural, needing no monitor to assure that you're performing in just the *right* way. These are not words of judgment. We all do this. These are words of learning, so that we can all move toward being authentic, which is our most natural and powerful state.

Our lives are largely run by the things on which we focus. And we have complete and ultimate authority over where our focus and attention are placed. So theoretically we should be able to connect with and influence others in every case. It is our choice. Does that make it simple? Yes. Is it easy? No. Why? Because we're dealing with fear. And that, it would seem, makes it all the more important to guard ourselves.

Scientific theory supports the significance of "attention" - in where and how we place it. If we place our attention on fear, that's what is further cultivated. Science explains this in relation to brain function. Neurological research has shown that the number of neurons firing in our brain increases depending on the strength of the attention, the focus we place on something.[2] One of the researchers noted, "When you pay attention, cells aren't only responding more strongly to that stimuli, a population of cells is responding more coherently."

She clarified that this meant responding in a more *organized* manner, "It is almost like the conductor stepping in to control a large set of unruly musicians in an orchestra so that they all play together. Cells synchronize precisely to the conductor's cues."[2,3]

Conversely, other research showed that when the subjects' attention was only partially on an object, the amount of information accurately processed and recalled, and the level of perception related to that object are limited to nonexistent. This latter dynamic was aptly named "inattentional blindness" by the researchers.[4,5]

Now this split-focus problem is about to get shocking. One of the studies on "inattentional blindness" shows how we can "notice" something, even look directly at it, without perceiving it at all.[5] In this research, Simons and Chabris did a revealing experiment in which they showed participants a short film of people playing basketball and asked them to count the number of times the ball was passed. While they were watching the film of people passing the ball, a person in a gorilla suit walked across the court in full sight. Forty-six percent of those watching, almost half, did not see the gorilla. They missed the gorilla! The research concludes that even when we're looking right at something, split-focus jeopardizes seeing it at all. So whatever is in our peripheral awareness is likely to be misperceived at best, and at worst, not seen at all.

This research has profound implications for my work. As described earlier, our lives are run by the things on which we focus. If we're focused on fear, it's as though we literally stoke the fire of fear in ourselves. That's where our awareness is.

At the same time, we've unplugged our brains from the message, from the interaction and from ourselves. So we become disconnected, our pathway cut off. And our diminished level of awareness greatly compromises our ability to fully process, comprehend, perceive and recall details. As we look on from a distance, through the eyes of fear, our view of the entire situation is distorted. So we're effectively not there at all. We're absent.

> *Turning Point*
>
> When we focus on fear, it is the *only* thing that exists.

We're no longer available for engagement or connection, and any expression of us as an authentic person has disappeared. We're hidden. As we focus on fear, we cease to be available in any meaningful way. And we've chosen it. It's not necessarily our conscious intention. It's just such a habit that we slip out even when we're not nervous. We all do it. And this research shows, whether we leave as a result of fear or not, the outcome is the same. The lights are on, but nobody's home!

This is exactly why multi-tasking is not only inefficient, it's often detrimental and even potentially dangerous. As the name implies, we are focused between two or more tasks. Now, if none of those tasks hold great significance for you and you can accept having limited comprehension and recall of each of them, then multi-tasking might be just the thing. And there are tasks like that for all of us, maybe taking out the trash while you listen to music on your headphones, for example.

But what about if you're in the hospital and a nurse is starting you on IV antibiotics while he's watching the football game on the overhead television. If his focus is between the IV and the game, where exactly is his attention when he's inserting a needle in your arm? Is he seeing your arm at that moment? We can only hope. And what about earlier that same day when you told the person taking your medical history that you have violent allergic reactions to penicillin? Were they doing two things at once? Did they even hear you?

A colleague shared the story of accompanying her 85-year-old mother to the doctor's office. While the doctor was intently making notes in her chart, he casually asked his patient how she'd been doing. So what followed was a story of how she'd been upset recently because her oldest brother, who raised her after the death of their father, had recently died. The doctor never stopped writing as she lamented how she was unable to attend his memorial service, which, she said, was very upsetting. Still making notes without looking up, the doctor commented, "Well, worry is what some of us do." Then, briefly glancing up at her, he offered, "And that's alright, it's just the way some people are." And the woman sat there with a puzzled look. That was a total disconnect from everything while the doctor was doing what seemed to be harmless multi-tasking.

Turning Point

I can effectively focus on only *one* thing at a time.

Now as a practical matter, some things must be "multi-tasked." Choose carefully.

I remember the day I was working with a big star who had just returned from one leg of his tour and wanted to talk about something that had happened the night before. He said, "I finished my show and was backstage in a small room where I was signing autographs for fans. This room had two doors, one from the arena where fans were lined up, and an exit door to the alley. I had been signing for about two hours," he said, "when my manager said speed it up because there was still a long line of people waiting. So I stopped talking with each person and just signed my name and looked up at them as I handed them the 8 x 10 picture. But that didn't speed things up enough, so finally I just kept my head down and signed as fast as I could. Now, what happened next freaked me out. They began to stack up against the walls all around this little room. I was handing everyone a signed picture and they would take it and just stand there. So finally, no one else could get in the room, and none of us knew what to do. Nobody said anything, they just stood there and wouldn't leave. It was freaky. And I don't know what went wrong."

Now, having read to this point in the book, you may know the answer to this artist's question. Point is, he should've known the answer too, but he didn't. So I asked him why anyone in their right mind would wait two or three or four hours to get his autograph. And we both laughed. "It's not the ink they wanted," I said. And he laughed again, but with a confused look on his face. "Did they really wait that long just for your autograph?" I asked. And I reminded him that everyone in that line already had his CDs and probably pictures too. "They waited in that line for you," I told him, "not for the ink from your pen. They wanted to feel as though they had met you and connected with you. Then that autograph would have reminded them of the thrill in that moment of connection." He was nodding by this time. "One last thing," I said. "It doesn't take but a second. You can connect instantly. You don't have to say anything, and that moment can hold such a powerful brightness that it will never be forgotten." He nodded and told me a story of having seen Springsteen on stage once. He said, "Wild horses couldn't have kept me from running backstage when that show was over. I had to see him." Then he smiled, "And I just wanted one thing. I wanted to feel like we had hooked up for just a second or two. He shook my hand and looked me in the eye. Didn't say a word. I'll never forget it."

It's not about the amount of time we spend with people. It's not about the words we say. *It's about where we choose to place our focus.* It's about whether we're connected with them for a moment.

One forever moment! People are starving for that connection, and it's not an easy thing to find. So when it happens, it matters. It's like lightning.

Fran learned it, but later. For now, her habit was to focus on how well she was coming across. Was it charming enough, Southern girl-next-door enough, smart or funny enough, and was it "whatever they wanted" enough? She did that mostly when the stakes were highest, times when her dream was on the line and she wanted it to be perfect. This is how Fran became invisible. If they could have really met Fran, not for the instrument she is, but for the completely wonderful person she is, it would have turned out differently. And it all happened because of where Fran chose to put her focus.

Turning Point

Fear, tricky as it is, always makes

itself available to us.

But we only become available to it

if we focus on it!

Past...Present...Future

One of the most powerful ways we use focus as a means of protection is in our shifting it between what we just did...what we're about to do – and what we're doing right now. How often do you take that trip? We all do it multiple times every day. We slide backward to dredge up recent memory of something we just said that we thought was really stupid. And we skip forward searching for just those perfect words to say next. In the process, we've left the interaction and retrieved the particular rule that's necessary for us to judge ourselves. And, throughout our entire trip between back and forth, we're still talking *now*.

The research on attention supports the power of this fear-based shift of focus between time zones. Not only does it render us available to past rules and judgment, it jeopardizes our ability to hear the words we're saying. And so, we're disconnected from the experience and the message. Ralph Waldo Emerson captures this tragedy, "What lies behind us and what lies before us are tiny matters compared to what lies within us." Our focus holds immeasurable power.

"But if I don't think ahead to figure out what I want to say," you ask, "then how will I know what to say?"

Here's exactly the way one client expressed her concern, "If I don't go out and get the words to say, I'm afraid the train will be gone and I won't be on it." It's a major fear. We worry that we'll either totally forget what to say or that we'll say something inappropriate to the situation.

A colleague in nursing education told me about a nursing student who insisted that while patients were talking to her, she absolutely had to "think ahead" to what her response would be. Otherwise, she feared saying the wrong thing and looking incompetent. I wondered what vital piece of patient information that student may have missed by tuning out.

A classic example came up recently as I worked with an artist who is a very successful singer and songwriter. He said, "The only time I forget the words to a song is when I'm worried about forgetting the words to the song. And they're my words. I wrote them." He described perfectly the shift away from what he was singing, as he worried about forgetting the words he was about to sing. And of course, he forgot the words. He was worrying instead of focusing on the lines he was singing in each moment. So when it was time to sing the verse he usually forgot, he forgot it. Why? As the attention research shows, it was because he was focused on the fear of forgetting and that was his reality in that moment, making him effectively absent from the words of the song. He made the choice and placed his focus.

~ Ironically, if you worry that you won't know the right thing to say, you won't - because you're not there to know what the right thing is. ~

Why? Because you've "checked out" worrying about it, and you've traveled into the future to find it or to plan it. You're focused on the fear, and for all practical purposes, you have removed yourself from the interaction. And like the songwriter, it becomes a self-fulfilling prophecy. Also, if you're not there, not only do you have difficulty remembering what to say, you can't hear what it is that you *do* say.

Absent-minded? That's an apt description. It has everything to do with focus.

SO WHAT ABOUT *ME?*

THINK ABOUT A "TYPICAL" DAY OF INTERACTIONS.

- ARE YOU MOSTLY IN THE PAST OR IN THE FUTURE? WHAT PERCENTAGE OF YOUR TIME IS IN EACH?
- THINK OF ONE OR TWO PEOPLE WITH WHOM YOU'RE COMFORTABLE ENOUGH TO JUST "BE."
- THINK OF SEVERAL PEOPLE YOU'RE NOT COMFORTABLE WITH. HOW ARE THEY DIFFERENT?
- WHAT WAS YOUR SENSE OF BEING CONNECTED OR DISCONNECTED IN INTERACTIONS WITH EACH?

Which portion of hyper-space, past, present or future, do you think our friend Fran lived in? Exactly right. Fran did it all. She went from past to future, then back to the past and so on. She may have slowed down a little while moving through *present* but she didn't stop there as she was observing and judging her performance during label auditions. In the first chorus, she wondered if the highlights in her hair were light enough. In the second verse, she questioned her posture. And between songs, she worried over a word choice she was trying to remember. Then, as the next song began, she went forward to prepare for the coming high note, then back to the past just after the high note to kick herself for missing it. And while we're giving Fran a hard time right now, the truth is that she's no different than the rest of us. This is a snapshot of what we all do. Our cautionary tactics really are exhausting. It's amazing that we don't get dizzy. It's also amazing that we ever actually get to know each other at all. Or do we?

Do you ever commit those perfect words to memory? What do you think you have to do in order to retrieve those memorized words? Yes, you have to go out into future search mode. As you're saying the first several words for example, your attention goes out to find the next few words. Once you've found them, you'll begin saying them as you launch your focus back into the future for the next sentence, and so on. Realize that you would be searching while you're talking, which means you would be completely absent. The result? You likely did say the words you memorized, and they might have been absolutely beautiful words. But since you were absent while saying them, they were almost certainly flat and lifeless. You weren't in them. They were just sounds. And if they were the perfect words, they were still sounds without life, without you. We believe and hope that memorizing a talk will keep us safe from judgment. But, since you must be absent to retrieve those memorized words, it succeeds only in keeping you focused in the future and absent in the present. Reading from a manuscript operates in much the same way.

Getting the content right is obviously important. And we're often taught that the words are the only thing of importance. If that were so, we could write it and read it, or for that matter we could write it and hand it out. The truth is that words spoken in absence are similar to words on a page. We may know more after hearing or reading those words, but will we be persuaded? The answer is, probably not, at least as it compares to the same words delivered well. It's not the answer you want to hear, but it may be the answer we all need to hear. Much more about this later.

Now, a quick note about the listener in these interactions. Much of the above applies, and there's an interesting twist. While the *other person* is talking instead of listening, we skip ahead to calculate what we might say back to them. We're planning the absolute *perfect* response. A colleague described that dynamic as "trumping." It fits. It's going out to grab the better phrase, the more convincing argument, or our proof that we've done something bigger or better than the person speaking. Trumped! So we're absent with our attention placed on something that isn't happening. We've checked out! And as the attention research shows, in reality, it's our comprehension and perception of what's really happening that get trumped.

The Power of Disconnection

Disconnection is a practical thing if it's what you choose to do. The problem comes when it seems to happen *to* you and there's no awareness of how it happened. And it's a very powerful thing. You're "out" and the other person is mad. Or you're out and the other person is hurt. Or you're out while your words would seem to be paying them a compliment, and the other person is confused. Or you're out and your life seems to be on auto-pilot with a sort of numbness where your feelings used to be. The result is that you're not in the room, and while your words could potentially at least inform your listener, that would depend on whether they're out since your being out removes any holding power the moment might have potentially had. So they're probably sitting there with their focus split and their attention somewhere else. And who is left?

If you choose to pull the plug, all of your focus drains away to somewhere else and so, while you're looking straight at someone, you fail to see them. And, yes, everyone knows you're gone. Everyone knows because everyone does it too, and they recognize it when they see it. They won't know what to call it, but they surely see it, and in that moment, they learn what it feels like.

If one person is a stone wall, the other person is likely to be absent too. And when person number one, who isn't aware he's made of stone, sees person number two turning to stone, then he solidifies a little more. And the insanity of this downward spiral picks up speed, each thinking it's the other.

Turning Point

How can you create the reality you want

if you're not there to create it?

Here's a classic "disconnect" story from a business associate of mine who ran into an acquaintance in a department store, a woman she hadn't seen in months. After a hug, her acquaintance shared that she'd suddenly lost her husband a few months back and, on the edge of tears, she whispered, "He was my best friend." My associate agonized as she recalled her response. Without hesitation, she blurted out, "Are you doing okay?" She was trying so hard to say just the right thing, just what her friend needed to hear...just what she should say. But being focused on her own discomfort rather than connecting with the other woman and her grief, my associate's mind immediately went in search of the perfect response. And since there is no perfect response in that case, she panicked and came back with, "Are you doing okay?" They were words disconnected from the situation. And her friend's answer let her know it, saying, "No, I'm not okay! I'm not okay at all!" My associate flushed and stared at the floor as the woman fought back tears. It was a simple example of how, by not trusting ourselves, we sabotage ourselves. My associate was afraid of being judged inadequate, and the fear of saying the wrong thing led her to say the wrong thing. That fear robbed them both of a desperately needed connection.

Whether it's an acquaintance, your best friend, a small gathering of co-workers, your child, your boss, 10 people around a table at a formal dinner party, a jury, a client, your staff of 50 or an audience of a thousand, if you're "checked out," you're immediately disconnected. You become invisible, and you are nowhere to be found.

The Power of Misperception

I'm sure you've heard the adage, "Perception is everything." But it's misperception that gives us fits. It's the reason we each think others don't "get us," and it's a two-way street. If we're misread because we're absent, we're also misreading them...because we're absent. So no one is basing anything on reality. Predictably, that leads to misunderstandings about meanings of words, feelings, and reactions on both sides of the interaction. Not only might we misperceive someone's body language, such as a shrug or a certain facial expression, we might literally not see it at all. It's just that our faculties of discernment cannot be active if we aren't focused.

The other side of misperception is that our absence leaves a blank page on which people can misperceive us. When we're unplugged, we aren't allowing them to get a read on us, and so their conclusions will be based on nothing concrete at all. But the blanks will be filled in, possibly with things like, unfriendly, aloof, shy, cold, uncaring or distant.

Also, in our absence, we're likely to give *mixed messages*, creating incongruence between *what* we say and *how* we say it. If people are absent and disconnected, they likely won't experience the emotion of their words. Have you seen someone deliver sad or even tragic news with a smile on their face? Or tell someone they're sorry using high-pitched notes? Or congratulate a colleague for a "job well done" in a bored tone? Or speak words that are meant to be moving and touching with no level of passion whatsoever. Mixed messages represent the epitome of misperception.

One of the most profound consequences of misperception is the erosion of trust. If the meaning of our words is ambiguous and we're nowhere to be found, what are they to believe? Who are they to trust?

What Might You Have Missed?

The truth is, in your absence, you might have missed just about everything that matters. How can you be in touch with your emotions if you're absent? And if you aren't in touch with how you feel, how can you convey your feelings to someone else? How can you tap into your passion? How can you fill them with any level of excitement or inspiration; how can you influence, persuade and move them if you're speaking empty words? How can you convey the experience of your message? It can't be done.

You're missing a large part of your life. How can you matter if you're not there? You're missing you!

Turning Point

If *you are* absent, the room will be empty,

whatever size the crowd.

Here's the Key:

It's with our thoughts, concepts and words that we inform.

It's in the delivery of that content that we influence and persuade.

And it's our presence that builds a bridge to the listener.

The Power of 93/7

Surprising findings arose after a study was published in the 1960s by Albert Mehrabian and Susan Ferris. They found that the words held only a 7% value as compared to the delivery of those words having a 93% value. Included in the 93% were voice, body movements and gestures.[6,7]

This research demonstrates the surprising power of delivery. It doesn't insinuate that the message is unimportant, but it does show the relative power of the way in which the message is delivered.

My take on these percentages is that the numbers are so high because it's all about presence. The reason the delivery is of such great importance is that it's the primary way you become visible. You can spout off a string of exciting and compelling words, but if you're absent the words have no life or passion or emotion. They fall flat and hollow.

A classic example of this occurred during the historic first-televised Presidential debate in 1960. The candidates were Senator John Kennedy and Vice President Richard Nixon. There's some background information from reporters coming up, but first let's set the scene. Kennedy was a fairly new member of Congress in his forties. Nixon was an experienced politician who as Vice President had made a name for himself as a foreign policy expert. And so the expectation was that Nixon would defeat the youngster with ease. That is, it was the expectation before the now famous debate.

The debate was in the day of black-and-white television, and it was before politicians had become aware of the manner in which perceptions were developed through the lens of a camera.

So the story goes from some reporters who were there, John Kennedy made a phone call to Nixon the day before the debate. He told the Vice President that he, Senator Kennedy, was not even considering wearing all that thick disgusting pancake makeup that some people wore on-camera. He told Nixon that he thought men in makeup looked ridiculous. And Vice President Nixon muttered something about not being seen in public wearing make up. The next day when the two candidates arrived at the hall for the debate, guess which one had on make up? Yes, it was Kennedy. Now, if you've been in a television studio, you know the sheer power of those very bright hot lights. Anyone who appeared under those lights without makeup looked as though they were sweating because the lights made their skin look shiny. And that was the beginning of a perception of Richard Nixon as a backroom politician who was nervous, sweaty, un-presidential, and who had a very strong five o'clock shadow as though he hadn't shaved in several days.

Now, that alone didn't win Senator Kennedy the debate. But that coupled with the fact that Kennedy looked tan and confident, and was serene, knowledgeable and presidential definitely put him over the top. He was *present*. And everyone who watched the debate now looked at John Kennedy as the obvious next President.

But here's the best part. Eric Sevareid was a bureau chief for CBS in Europe during that time and he was reporting from there the next day. Remember, there were no satellites then and no live television. So Sevareid didn't see the debate, he read about the debate in a morning newspaper and he read the transcript - every word.

He began his report by saying that the obvious debate winner was Richard Nixon, that he had more information, stated it from a place of experience, and was obviously the more knowledgeable candidate. It was no contest, according to the reporter who had read the text of the debate. And Americans who had only read about it firmly agreed. They all read the same words that TV viewers had heard, but they couldn't see the candidates nor hear their voices. They had only 7%.

Now, in truth, John Kennedy was present, passionate, powerful and looked presidential as he sat there in his makeup. But even though it makes a good story, it wasn't the makeup. Oh, Nixon did himself no favor by stepping on the set all pasty white and looking nervous. But, had he been able to be present during that debate, it might have had an entirely different outcome since he would have been working with more than just the 7%.

Turning Point

When you're the focus of attention, a step into

self-consciousness could have you *acting*

like something you're not.

Chapter Four

A Disappearing Act:
Widening the Target

◇ By choosing to act...I have taken the path of fear ◇

Playing a role in order to meet someone's preconceived standards is a common but difficult thing to do. Trying to be someone you're not isn't easy. Most of us are terrible actors. Yet we act much of the time, when we're fearful, self-conscious, wanting to avoid judgment or seeking to be accepted. We settle into it, so to speak, and lose sight that we're doing it. When we're acting, we're looking at the world through the eyes of fear, so we lose sight of much that's reality. An ancient wisdom in the Talmud captured this, "We do not see things as they are, we see them as we are." We even have tools we use to cement our acts in place. And, then, the more we do it, the more we seem to achieve new heights of control. We're told it's safer.

Remember that as part of our indoctrination into society, we're bombarded with expectations like, "Act more like your brother."..."Act like a lady."..."Act your age."..."Act like a man!"..."Act right!" We're ordered to act. So we do it and we preach it, but we don't like it when someone does it to us. We see through their act immediately. Why? Because we do it, so we recognize it when it's done to us. Everyone recognizes it. They may not know what to call it, but they spot it every time. We are unintentionally taught that acting is safer than just being ourselves. We are taught to copy and to conform. And those who taught us thought it was safer. This is not done to cause harm. Yet it causes harm.

> *Turning Point*
>
> Arising from fear, acting propels us
>
> into an ever-widening fear spiral.

It's no accident that the "mask" has become a symbol of disguise. And it seems to work well in allowing us something to hide behind. Please know that there's no judgment intended by my offering the idea that we all wear masks from time to time. And I suggest that finding our mask will help us make progress toward the eventual goal of authenticity and personal power.

Masquerading is No Ball

We've said that this masquerade typically begins in early childhood and often becomes a pervasive behavior. In order to convey a compelling act, the accompanying mask is useful. We shape it and sculpt it. And we practice it and hone its appearance. Strangely, we seldom question or abandon our masks. In fact, the real danger of the mask is that we can forget it exists and sometimes believe that we *are* our mask.

From my work with several thousand clients, I've isolated the common acts and their mask extensions. They "seem" to provide practical tools needed for survival in dealing with other people.

The 'JOKER' Mask

I remember the moment I learned it was possible for someone to think they were their act or mask. I was doing a seminar for bank executives with seven or eight vice presidents in a conference room. Each time I touched on a topic that made one particular man uncomfortable, he would throw out a glib, witty remark. The first time, everyone laughed; then as it continued, they just looked over at him without any comment. When it was time for the group to learn about acting and masks, I spoke to this particular executive, who we'll call John, and gave him an assignment. I did my best to be reassuring so as not to make him feel under a spotlight. I said, "John, I want you to do something for me. For the next 10 minutes, I want you to drop the funny, witty lines. Just for 10 minutes. I want to show you something." Now, what happened next taught me a crucial lesson. Here's what John did. He looked straight at me, not saying a word, and his face got pale. He was very wrapped up in whatever he was thinking. The whole room waited. Finally John asked, "But if I stop doing that, who will I be?" And I got it. John thought he was his mask. He was so earnest with his question that the veins in his neck stood out, as he repeated, "Who will I be?"

Once he stopped being the joker for 10 minutes, John had a brief taste of life without playing that role. And there was freedom in that awareness. For John, what began as a simple act to relieve his tension ended with a realization that he was not that.

The next part is tough to explain. When John stopped for 10 minutes, he first seemed confused, and then he seemed relieved. For the next hour, he would catch himself doing it again, and he would make himself stop. Finally, the mask was completely gone. And this is the part I don't quite have words for; the rest of the group almost took a collective sigh of relief that John was back. They wouldn't have said that, but they seemed to feel it. Something about John had been missing. And when he returned, the group breathed.

There was another 'joker' moment, this one in a seminar with about 16 people who were working on communication skills. One man, we'll call him Marty, was making sure to establish his position not so much as the funny guy, but as the strange guy. Everything about him was unusual, colorful and screamed for attention. He took the role of joker seriously, as though he deserved to be stared at and laughed at - and not in a good way. He said as much. So here is a bright, capable, successful man who sees himself as none of that.

When his turn came to talk to the group, he stood up and proposed a task. Everyone in the room was to say how they saw him within a "Gilligan's Island" scenario. Did they see him as Gilligan? As the rich guy? Perhaps as Mary Ann? He laughed out loud at the thought. Or finally, did they see him as the Professor? The room became very still. No one laughed, even when he asked if they saw him as Mary Ann. Silence. More silence. So he turned to me and said, "Okay, Jeri, would you see me as Gilligan?"

Now if you could meet this wonderful man, you would never imagine that he would actually see himself as Gilligan. But his joker mask, to him, looked like Gilligan. His hair was funny, his socks were loud, and he dressed the Gilligan part.

I waited for someone to step in. Silence. Finally someone said, "Marty, hard as you try, you are clearly not Gilligan. And just as clearly, you're not Mary Ann." Everyone laughed. Someone else stepped forward and very solemnly asked the group, "How many of you see Marty as the Professor?" Every hand went up. Marty looked around the room and slumped to the floor, his legs no longer able to hold him up. He was so shocked that not one person believed his act...and it literally disappeared in that moment.

The next day when Marty walked into the

meeting room, he looked entirely different. No funny hair, no loud clothing and no Gilligan mask. All of it was gone, as though it had never been.

These are examples of freedom coming in the form of awareness. When John and Marty had the opportunity to evaluate life with the mask compared to life without it, they realized they were not their masks.

So, as you see, the person wearing the joker mask acts glib, witty, humorous, and clever when under pressure. The pressure, regardless of the mask, goes by the same name. It's always fear.

Before we explore the remaining masks, let me be certain that you clearly understand I am not labeling you. You are not a mask or an act. That's the whole point. As we name these masks, you may recognize one as a tool you have used at one time or another. You may even see a mask that you use regularly. My enduring goal is for you to realize that you are so much more than any mask or act. And yet, if you can recognize the masks for what they are, it is then possible to raise your awareness to the point that you will no longer have need of them. The point is that you do not now nor have you ever needed a mask. This book is dedicated to proving that point.

The 'SHY' Mask

This very common mask also goes by the names loner, wallflower or introvert. This is the person who wants to disappear into the woodwork and become invisible. The shy notion is often confirmed by those who went into their personality test feeling shy and came out labeled an introvert. If we believe it, then we exhibit it as though it's so whether or not it really is. This is the person who literally shies away from taking certain jobs, accepting certain promotions or attending certain social events. In other words, anything that might require them to step into the limelight. I want those of you who think of yourself as shy to consider something. Shy is a word. So is joker. You would never say someone has a disability and it's called being a joker. Yet you may think of yourself as being less capable than others because you're shy. Sometimes jokers are funny. Sometimes they're not. Sometimes you feel shy. Sometimes you don't. You're shy or not shy depending on the situation. Loosen your grip on identifying yourself as shy. Remember we're talking about masks. Just something to consider. There is so much freedom in the realization that you don't have to act shy.

The 'PERFECTIONIST' Mask

This is the mask of a person who goes to extremes being careful to do it exactly right, whatever "it" is. We are trained to prepare by writing our words so we can either read them, or so we can memorize them and spit them out exactly as written. That is our version of doing it exactly right. Then, we reason, we won't mess up and say the wrong thing, and we won't freeze up and look stupid, and we won't lose our place and be embarrassed. Problem is, the perfectionist is very likely to cause the three things he is most afraid of. But this is what we're taught to do; and so when it doesn't work time after time, we try harder time after time.

The truth is we've been taught the wrong thing. Reading a manuscript or memorizing a manuscript can't lead to perfection. This mask is designed to put up a perfect front. It relies entirely on the words and the information they convey. It insists that the message is the only thing and that if you get the message exactly right, you will succeed. We've been taught the wrong thing. The message informs. The delivery is the primary agent of persuasion and clarity. But even with that you must be engaged during the delivery. So there is a method of getting to perfect, but this isn't it.

The 'PROFESSOR' Mask

This is the professorial role, the mask of a person who lives mostly in their head. They make their home in their intellect because they believe they should. The professor speaks largely in theoretical terms. He analyzes and postulates in place of feeling and experiencing. In interactions, he might tend toward an examination of the concepts, using formal, strategically oriented and non-conversational words.

Sometimes, the professor mask can arise out of a need to meet outside expectations as in the following story.

A senior pastor I was coaching was holding tightly to a beautifully sculpted professor mask. He did it with the most honorable intention. This minister had been preaching in Florida for two decades, moving from church to church with great success. He was respected, bright, and seen as a leader. Then one day he got a phone call from his regional supervisor telling him that he was being moved to the "high steeple" church in the capital city. It was a promotion. "And oh, by the way," bragged the supervisor, "almost all the university professors attend that particular church."

Now, this pastor, prior to that phone call, was known for his ability to make lasting personal connections with members of his church from the pulpit. He was making a difference in their lives through his sermons, which was a major reason for his promotion. But it was about to be left behind as he moved to his new church.

He stopped what had made him successful so that he could start what was expected of him. Now, this was a self-imposed expectation that he should become professorial. It seemed common sense that he should try to match his congregation. And without his conscious knowledge, the professor mask was born.

He worked at it. He spent hours crafting the sermon, double-checking for grammar and word definitions. And then he proudly read that sermon verbatim from the very tall pulpit that hung 15 feet in the air at the front of the huge sanctuary. It felt strange doing it that way, but he wanted to meet their expectations. The words were perfect and he read the beautifully. But as Sundays came and went, something was going terribly wrong. For the first time in his career, the attendance went down instead of up. So he worked harder, polished his work to be even more professorial, worked on improving his vocabulary and did everything he thought would be appropriate to his new church. Nothing changed for the better during the ensuing six-month period.

One day he got a phone call asking him to come back to his old church for one Sunday sermon while their new pastor was away. So he took a Sunday off, feeling he needed a break from the pressure anyway. And when he stepped into that pulpit, the magic returned. He had done no preparation for the sermon to speak of. He simply chose the topic, jotted down three points on a card, thought of a couple of stories and delivered. The sermon lasted 20 minutes and when he said the last word, the congregation stood up and applauded. There were some tears.

Later that night, he asked his wife a question that he had been afraid to ask before, "Why isn't it working in our new church, when it seems to so easily work here?" And she said, "Because you're different. You left yourself at your old church."

This story has a happy ending. It was completely turned around the very next week when he stepped up in front of his new church. He was standing in the center of the lower level, without a pulpit and without a manuscript. Here's what he said: "My dear friends, I have learned one of the great lessons of my life over the past two weeks. I have realized that

I was trying to impress you rather than to just be myself, which would have been impressive enough because it has become so rare. I have hidden behind this pulpit and behind these fancy words, instead of being myself and allowing you to experience the deep feelings that I have for the work that I do. I have pretended that what you need and want on Sunday morning is to have me talk to your minds. I think I did that. And it didn't work, and it can't work because that isn't why you're here. I have realized that we're all here because we're hungry for something real, something that we can experience together, something that can help us make it through next week. And I want you to hear this promise from me to you. I will not hide from you or leave you again. I will be here in front of you even if what I offer is raw and imperfect. I will be real with you. That is my promise."

It has been several years since that day; and his church, large as it had been, is now much larger. And people still talk about the day their pastor walked down from the pulpit and into their hearts.

The 'IRONMAN' Mask

This mask is related to the professor in that it's built largely on expectation, but it looks different. The ironman mask is an executive-styled, seriously rigid, highly controlled metal business machine. Male or female, young or old, the ironman is a boss machine. It may be sophisticated, it may be blue collar, the language and dress may vary, but the boss is the boss.

This is one of those masks that becomes body armor. It's really hard to fit yourself into it, because it seems so unlike everything you are. But once you buckle yourself into the boss armor, it's extremely difficult to get out. This one is a full-on, head-first act that you lock on in the morning and then throw off when you get home at night...or perhaps not.

It's not a natural way of dealing with colleagues. So, if we think we have to throw orders around, then there's only one way to do it and that is to disappear behind the iron mask.

This one is exhausting. It takes massive energy to keep this mask alive, which makes it all the more strange that it often becomes permanent once we forget that it's a mask and not us.

The 'HAPPY FACE' Mask

This is the mask for the person who perpetually, regardless of circumstances and even under the most adverse conditions, has a smile on their face. If it were an authentic expression of a positive attitude even in the face of adversity, that would be one thing. But this is about the person who feels the need to display an incessantly chipper and perky look and behavior. It is similar to the joker in that we choose to "put on a happy face" as a means of avoiding worry or pain. This mask is particularly obvious because the conveyed emotion consistently conflicts with circumstances.

Of the thousands of clients I've worked with over 30 years, almost every one fits somewhere in the dynamic of one or more of these masks, either out of their own perceived needs or their preconceived expectations. We each have our favorite.

~ Ironically, the mask is an attempt to escape fear, yet it creates a disconnect which, then, perpetuates the fear. ~

Playing the Part

These masks and the acts that accompany them are neither good nor bad. They are simply tools that we unknowingly develop over the years. It is the awareness that they exist which is the key to stepping away from their allure.

So to clarify, various roles and realities are a part of our lives. Of course, you are a daughter when you're with your mother. But that is you being a daughter, not acting like one. And if you're the boss at work, then you are being the boss because that is your reality. But if you have the "boss" title and yet you're acting like a tyrant because you believe it is expected of you, then you are not *being*, you are acting.

So, as I advise my clients, what you must do is to be yourself within the roles and responsibilities you accept into your life. We all wear a number of hats. The real you doesn't change because you change your hat.

"Well," you ask, "if we're such bad actors how do we pull it off anyway?"

You accomplish that by using creative tools to block out everything that is not the act. Let me show you.

When "Skills" Become Blocks

Now, this is the point at which we begin to manufacture tools to fit the task. If the task is to cement the act in place, then we develop a favorite tool to do the job. This is not something you now have to do consciously. You did this long ago. This section is designed to assist you in spotting the tools you already use to hold your act firmly in place. Again, let me say that this is not a judgment, just a statement of fact for most people. Not bad, just reality. I'm hoping that if we can stop judging ourselves, perhaps we can take a look at the dynamics that are successfully separating us from one another.

The favorite "blocks" seem to be a set of skills by which we deliver what we say. They're not the only ones, just the most popular. I refer to this dynamic as "blocking" because it solidifies your act or mask by blocking you from being real. And, in that way, it's a primary mechanism for mixed messages.

So what does that mean? It means if your block is *volume*, you will speak much louder as you talk about something you don't wish to feel. In that example, the loudness is the tool by which you separate yourself from the reality of your feelings. It keeps you from being in touch. It's a separation tool, and the problem is that it works. It can also be confusing for a listener. For example, if you're talking loud to disengage from the painful experience you're describing, your listeners are hearing you speak in very loud terms about something that they expect to be spoken very softly. Or, the block could be a mid-level volume when speaking about anger. Again, a mismatch between the meaning of the words versus the delivery.

So we are making the choice to set up these powerful blocks. We choose the situation in which we block what is real. If we realize we are choosing, we are in control of it. If the habit of blocking is used unaware, then it's in control of us, resulting in the desired inability to engage.

Let's look at the mechanics of engaging another person so that we can see how this works. *Voice tone* is the notes on which we speak. It is the primary means of conveying how we feel about what we say. And there's a code. Higher tones mean enthusiasm, excitement, pride or joy. Lower tones communicate serious, sad, or concerned feelings. And interestingly, if you are stuck on the one or two notes in the middle, you are likely perceived as apathetic. So to use voice tone as a blocking mechanism would be to lock in on that central note and thus remove yourself from experiencing what you're saying. Or you might hit higher notes when talking about a painful subject. Doing that would successfully keep you from feeling the words. It would also create a mismatch for your listener between what you described as being painful and saying it with high notes.

Another skill commonly used as a block is *emphasis*, which is the mechanism for clarifying the meaning of what we say. We emphasize by lifting a word or words out of the sentence with our voice, thus bringing it to the attention of the listener. To compare two things, for instance, we would emphasize both items so that they can be heard more clearly than the other words in that sentence. For example, "*Last quarter* sales were *down*, but *this quarter* sales were *up* 15%." Without the emphasis on both the time periods and the numbers, this sentence would have been unclear when spoken.

If emphasis were your blocking mechanism, you might omit it altogether. The problem is, without emphasis, it would be difficult to understand what you're saying. But it's a successful block, in that it keeps you absent and seemingly safe.

Here is a quick exercise that will illustrate the importance of emphasis as a clarifier of your meaning. Here is a sentence with 5 words: "She never said they lied." Take your time and read this sentence 5 times, each time you will emphasize the next word in the sentence. You will start by emphasizing the word "She." You can say it slowly to emphasize it. You might say it crisply or loudly. The way you do it isn't as important as that it calls attention to the word. Now read the sentence for the second time and emphasize the word "never." Keep this up and listen to the meaning of the sentence change as you emphasize the different words. It has the potential to completely change the meaning.

Pacing is the next skill. It is the speed at which we speak. We naturally speed up or slow down to match what we're saying, unless it is used as a "block." Then we lock in at a medium speed and that allows us to disengage.

A *speaking style* is often defined by the spacing and pausing within sentences or paragraphs. The style itself is often a block. An executive style, for example, would see words broken up into sections of three or four words each, with a long pause between each section. It is, by design, both controlled and cautious, thus being an effective block.

Level 1 and *Level* 2 are descriptive of the levels of content in communication. Think of Level 1 as facts and Level 2 as feelings and experiences. It is Level 1 on which we will focus as the potential blocking mechanism.

Level 1 refers to head stuff: who, what, where, and when. It is data such as figures, dates, times, and sizes. Level 1 is the primary information carrier. It informs. This is the level typically used in the corporate world, with "getting to the bottom line" being the common refrain. Only the facts seem necessary or expected in many cases. The problem comes when we need to do more than just inform, since a deeper level is needed for full persuasion.

Level 2 provides an *experience* of the data held at Level 1. Without the Level 2 experience, Level 1 operates almost exclusively in the gray matter. At this level, the sender thinks and informs...and the receiver thinks. Only at Level 2 does the receiver experience what is being said. Level 2 is the persuader since it conveys the feeling and experience of the content.

A Level 1 conversation over lunch, for example, is informative, since you will know more than you did before the lunch meeting. But if you add Level 2, then there is an experience of the person. At Level 1, I know *about* you. At Level 2, I *know* you.

Level 1 is such a strong "blocking mechanism" because it's good at keeping people in their heads, especially the speaker. To form a block using Level 1, you would stay away from stories and feelings and stick to the facts. That way, you can restrict yourself only to matters that affect the intellect. That will largely prevent you from experiencing what you say.

A classic Level 1 block was seen by millions during the Hurricane Katrina disaster when a doctor described losing many of his patients after they waited together on the hospital roof for help to arrive. And no help arrived. The doctor described only the medical procedures he did. It was kept completely technical and impersonal...data only. That is a Level 1 block. In this case, he probably felt it was the only way he could revisit those painful days without dissolving into sobs. But it was strange and confusing to watch because while his eyes showed the pain, there was a slight smile on his face as an additional hedge against his feelings...feelings that were kept silent.

Perhaps, in the listing of blocks, you spotted one that looked or felt familiar to you. If so, then we have come to an important point of awareness. These tools, all of them, the masks and acts and blocks are very common and they are usually plugged in without your being aware.

~ Ironically, our "blocks" block everything except what they were designed to block - our fear. ~

This is what I mean by "widening the target." From the attention research, we can see how, as we focus more of our attention on blocking and less on the interaction, our disconnect grows. We'll be seen as removing ourselves from the person with whom we are interacting. That can be misinterpreted as apathy, aloofness or arrogance. Thus, what seemed to us a protective device becomes, in the eye of a colleague or friend, a means of distancing ourselves from them. And in certain circumstances, this dynamic might explain why we are sometimes surprised when we expect a friendly encounter, and it turns confrontational.

CONSIDER THE INTERACTIONS YOU LISTED EARLIER.

- IN EACH ONE, REFLECT ON CONSISTENT PATTERNS. PERHAPS TERMS YOU USE TO DESCRIBE YOURSELF, FOR EXAMPLE, "I'M A SLOW TALKER," "I TEND TO SPEAK SOFTLY," "I'M NOT EXCITING, I SOUND FLAT," "I BACK PEOPLE AWAY WITH MY VOICE, IT'S SO LOUD" OR "I GET STUCK IN JUST THE FACTS."
- WRITE YOUR ANSWER.

Let's track these actions we've described and hook them together so that the dynamic becomes clear. First, we are anxious. Then we search for protection from that fear. We locate and use a means, a block, for distancing or removing ourselves from the interaction. And since we've removed our authentic self, we must now fill that gap with an act. When we act like something we are not and put on a mask, we're essentially absent from that interaction.

We're also absent from our own feelings that would naturally arise from the interaction. So, there is a mismatch, a lack of congruency between our words and the way in which they are delivered. Not only are we disconnected from our feelings about the words we are saying, but we often don't even hear the words we say. And so our message might seem inappropriate to the situation. This is a symptom of being absent. We have just described the tools by which we make that happen.

If we don't hear the words we say, and we aren't connected to the feelings congruent with the words... then we are absent. Although our warm body is standing right there and our eyes may be looking directly at the other person, we are disengaged. The same dynamic can happen with gestures. A motion, a step, a smile are all powerful when they are congruent with the words you are saying at the time. If not, they can be confusing.

When Fran, our artist, would "check out" she might sweep her hands upward in a triumphant gesture. Problem is, if Fran wasn't listening to the words she sang at the moment of her triumphant gesture, it could be entirely inappropriate. Why? Because Fran was absent and out of touch.

In any case, the result is that the message is misunderstood and that we are misunderstood. This could be why others don't seem to hear you, don't know who you really are, and don't know what you're really feeling.

And so you ask, "Discomfort or not, and even if it means acting, don't we all have to meet others' expectations at some point?"

No. Absolutely not! When we're talking about expectations relating to who you are, the answer is no! We've seen that acting like something you're not creates the opposite of the kind of success you really want. Our masks and parts we play only serve to eclipse our authenticity. But what really fulfills our dreams and fills our soul is connection, clarity and the freedom to be ourselves – for me to be *me.*

Now we have reached the time to reveal the means to be authentic. For me, it has been the path to freedom: *The Technology of Authentic Presence.*

Chapter Five

Presence:
The Essential Element

◊ There are several paths to presence...
but presence is the one path to authenticity ◊

Each of us has the right to live fully, to be present within our own lives. In fact, we must if we are to live free. If not, we are what is missing in our lives. And that is too painful to endure.

Presence is the light at the end of the tunnel. What has been missing in published theories on presence is a practical method that works in every type of interaction to maintain authenticity in our lives. What is offered here is that practical tool, one that interfaces with scientific research in the area of selected attention, and a method supported by over

30 years of actual fieldwork with many thousands of people. That fieldwork holds the assurance that this method will succeed.

Authentic Presence

The key to a problem often lies in its antithesis, like two sides of a coin. This makes it very clear what action we must take. Fortunately, such is the case for the fear within interactions that robs you of you, rendering you absent, disconnected, misperceived, limited and even more fearful in your personal and business lives. So, assuming we choose not to live in fear, why aren't we simply doing the opposite of that? Because we don't yet recognize fear as the problem, and if we did, we wouldn't believe that being fearless is within the realm of possibility. But it is indeed, and now we're going to go there together.

Authentic Presence is the door to you. The key to opening that door is the way in which we choose to focus our attention.

In the late 1800s, William James, the father of psychology, often spoke about attention as the mind "taking possession" of one out of many thoughts, a withdrawal from one thing in order to effectively handle something else. This taking possession is, in fact, our intentional focus.

The body of research on "selective attention" gives us insight into specific ways our focus determines whether that door is open or closed. These study findings support that anything less than a subject's *full* attention results in fewer neurons being fired and a compromised to nonexistent ability to process, perceive and recall information related to the object.[2,3,4,5] So, focus on fear and you're fearful, instantly igniting the spiral into disconnection and powerlessness.

Now, the *other* side of the coin: Full focus of attention on an object results in overall enhanced processing of information and more accurate perception and recall related to the object.[2,3,4,5] So, focus your full attention on the words and feelings in the interaction and you are fearless.

But are we really capable of directing our full attention or is it at the mercy of circumstance? Research on the topic reveals "The Cocktail Party Effect," which essentially finds that we are, in fact, capable of intentionally focusing our attention, for example, on just one voice above a din of voices at a cocktail party.[8] Moreover, the Moveable Filter Theory found that the earlier in an interaction one pays full attention, the greater the "attentive capacity," resulting in more accurate perception.[9] In other words, tune in early if you want to get an accurate read of what's going on.

These research findings on "attention" parallel the findings of my 30 years of field work and anecdotal findings on the mechanism and results of "selected attention" that I call *being present*. Being present is full focus on the words and feelings within the interaction.

Being present carries the enhanced ability to accurately comprehend and process information, leading to experiencing the feelings and meaning of the message and the interaction. It is connecting with ourselves first, so that we can connect with others. It is our *presence.* It's this connection that is the bridge for authentically sharing that experience. It becomes our *authentic presence.* And this is the key to fearlessness, pure and simple. You are unavailable to fear and so you have no self-consciousness. You are unavailable to judgment, at ease, connected, fully visible and unlimited. You are *authentic presence.*

The Technology of Authentic Presence

HOW IT WORKS

Authentic Presence begins with where we choose to focus our attention. Recall that when we're self-conscious, we're watching ourselves. Our focus is either out in the future gathering up the thing we'll say next, or we're in the past thinking about something we just said, probably to criticize it. Now remember, whether your focus is in the future or the past, you're talking in the "right now."

So here's the question: What's missing? What's missing is your attention and focus on what you're saying right now. With that clarification, you've just discovered the answer to fear.

Turning Point

The answer is to be "present."

To actually experience the words and the feeling of those words at the exact moment you speak them.

Not before, not after, but *exactly* as you say each word.

So how does that stop the fear cycle? First, for the sake of this lesson, let's oversimplify and say that our consciousness runs on one track so that our attention to one thing rules out our attention to anything else in a given moment. If we are focused on thing #1, and suddenly we shift our focus, then thing #1 is no longer there for us. We are now focused somewhere else. And so, if my one thought in this moment is about what I'm saying, I can't be focused on fear. My focus is preoccupied with a thought, and it's not the thought of being afraid. So I can't be afraid. I literally can't.

Second, my full attention has to be focused on something for it to be fully in my awareness. The result is that fear exists only if I'm focused on it. Only then am I available to be afraid. When I am self-conscious, I have chosen fear without even realizing it. But I do have a choice.

So, as I talk, if I hold only one thought

in each portion of a moment,

AND

if fear has only one doorway and that is via my focus on it,

THEN

where I focus my attention is the key to fear.

Here's the clear choice: Either focus on the fear and be afraid, or be present by focusing on the words and become fearless. It is one or the other, never both. It may seem to be both because our minds move so quickly back and forth between the words and the fear, but it cannot be both.

Therefore, focusing on fear becomes a choice, and with that, the potential for you to be in full control.

Presence is the pathway to living undisguised.

It requires the courage to allow people to really meet you as you both experience what it is that you're talking about. It places you, your passion, your convictions and your heart and feelings squarely in view of your listener. And it is the most powerful and compelling thing that you can do.

It is to actually experience the words and their inherent meaning as you say them. It enlivens a set of words, it is exciting, and it is real with the speaker remaining present and authentic. Have you ever been talking or telling a story and suddenly you become so enmeshed in the story as you actually relive the events, that you forget where you are, you forget the time, and you forget the listener as you fall into the message? That is being fully present. It is powerful because to be present is to be accessible. And as you talk, the listeners form their own visuals

---

and feelings of the events you are describing. They will even experience what you're talking about, but only if you're present. *So the gift is, if you are present they will likely be present too.* It becomes an experience that you actually give to the listener. They may not know how to hook in by themselves. But if you drop into being present first, then they can join you within a few seconds. It is irresistible.

No doubt, it's easier to be present under certain circumstances. If you're sitting down to dinner with a close friend and you get into an animated conversation, do you slip out into the future to find what you'll say next? Do you go into the past to criticize yourself about something you just said? Or do you just stay present and trust that what you say will be fine? Most of us cherish those moments with people we love and trust in which we are just ourselves. No pretense. No acting. We know through past experience that who we are is enough for those select few whom we hold dear for just that reason. Think about those people in your life who are dearest to you, whom you trust totally, whom you call good friends. Are they present when you talk about matters that are serious to you? Are they totally attentive, focusing their energy completely on you? Chances are, the answer is yes. That's likely why they're good friends. Now think of a few people whom you would call acquaintances. Can you picture their faces, their eyes, when you're talking with them? Are they mostly absent, with their attention coming and going? Again, chances are the answer is yes.

So, if we know how to be present in some circumstances, it is simply a matter of choice to be present in all circumstances. It isn't necessarily easy, but it can be done. Being present when you are interacting allows authenticity because you are experiencing what you're talking about as you say it. The combination of presence and authenticity creates power. A person who is willing to be present and, therefore, authentic is the most compelling and powerful of people. It is as irresistible as it is rare.

PRINCIPLE ONE: *Being present* is to be *fully* focused and to place that full focus on only *one* thing.

HOW IT WORKS

If you place your full focus on your own fear, then you have unplugged yourself from the interaction in front of you. Of course, you're still interacting, still talking, but that's not where your attention is. Whatever is getting your full focus is getting your full attention. And it's that which your brain best recognizes. So, if you focus on fear, fear is what is in your awareness.

Turning Point

My focus is my own. Will I choose
to focus on fear and be afraid?

PRINCIPLE TWO: Place your point of focus on that with which you want to connect.

Here's the question: "Am I aware of what I'm focused on, for the most part?" If the answer is "No," then you could easily be focusing on fear without knowing it. For example, since self-consciousness arises out of fear, when you're self-conscious, you've chosen to focus your attention on fear without realizing it. And about a million times a day, our minds roll around those cookie-cutter thoughts that we pretend we don't have, like: "I'm just fat" or "I know I will forget that second verse" or "I'm a true screw-up" or "I'm going to freeze and forget his name" or "I'm so lame" or "I know she doesn't notice me" or "I just know I'm going to fall up those stairs." That last one, "I just know I'm going to fall up those stairs" is something a client actually said to me as she was preparing to walk up a very long flight of stairs on a television award show set. She said it to me four times in the space of an hour, and I tried to point out to her that she was focused on something that she definitely did not want to occur on live television. So I watched that next night when she did win the award and she did walk up those stairs toward the microphone – and wouldn't you know it, she did trip and fall forward on her knees right there on national television...and, with a pained grin on her face, she did finally scramble up to the podium to accept her award.

It's more than mental practice when you hold something in your attention to the point of it being your exclusive focus. It is the thing that you are actually creating. It's astounding how powerful we are when we set our mind to it. Choose your point of focus carefully, as though what you desire to create will happen. Focus only on what you do want, never on what you don't. And never, ever focus on fear.

PRINCIPLE THREE: Being attentive is everything.

Being attentive is engagement and connection. It is memory and recall. It is intuition and accuracy in reading a situation or person. It is instant access to available input. It is the delivery system for influence. It is the solution to fear. And it is being present to give and receive love. If you are absent and I can't find you, I might still love you, but would you know? So giving full attention to what is in front of you is everything, because that allows you to be present in your life. Absent that, you're disconnected.

A Reversal of Misfortune

Being present breaks the downward spiral of fear. At this point, you are no longer just on the path to authentic presence. You have arrived. This is all about awareness. If all you do is read this book and never practice it or think about it again, you will soon make great progress. Why? Because you are now aware of the concepts surrounding presence and of their application and meaning. That awareness is more the answer than your practice or study. What is happening to you even now is the beginning of a spontaneous halting and reversal of every dynamic related to fear, self-consciousness, absence and acting. Feelings of discomfort are lessening. Your perceived need for disconnection is being reassessed. Misperceptions will decrease. There is no learning curve here. You are either fully present or fully absent. There is no partial presence. You're either fully aware of this technology and the truth of it, or you're fully unaware of it. And that matters.

If you will continue on this path of re-wiring your beliefs and practices, here is what will happen: You will live through an amazing transformation. You will live in the present moment much, even most of the time. You will be consumed by self-confidence rather than self-consciousness. And you will, with no apology at all, be everything that you are. And once you live in enough of your moments, you will see it. We are sometimes the last to know of our gifts and wonders. But you will know.

Turning Point

Your awareness is heightened. You know beyond any doubt that the act and mask you have hidden behind are not you.

———————————

You are the light at the end of the tunnel.

It's a long-awaited freedom. You are free to be who you *really* are, to drop all disguises all the time and to give the best you have to give. It's not the gift of what you say, so much as the gift of who you are. And when you're being present, you're available to yourself and to others, available to connect. You're *present* to your words and to their words. You're there to more accurately perceive your own and their feelings and to respond authentically.

All those elements of voice tone, emphasis, volume and pacing will perfectly match the words you speak and the emotion you feel. It's what people mean when they say someone is "a natural!"

We are halfway home. Presence requires the awareness of how and why we're absent in the first place, which you now possess. Secondly, it requires awareness that presence is the path to authenticity, which you now possess. Finally, it requires a comprehension of the paths to presence, the "how to" of The Technology of Authentic Presence. *Remember that even though there are several paths to presence, it only takes one to get you there.*

So, here we go. Being present is something you already do. You do it at times when you're not fearful and self-conscious. It's what makes your interactions work and allows you to be comfortable, while allowing others to "get you." It's just that we don't understand all the moving parts...yet.

Next, we're going to look at the specific tools to assist you in achieving presence. Any one of these transformational tools can instantaneously shift your focus into being present. It only takes one.

Let's Explore Ways of Being Present

The Definition:

BEING PRESENT IS INTENTIONALLY HOLDING YOUR FULL ATTENTION ON THE WORDS AS YOU SPEAK THEM AND ON YOUR EXPERIENCE OF THOSE WORDS.

The Implementation:

- **Point of Focus:** To hear and experience each word and its related feeling as you speak it. An intentional Point of Focus on the words and feelings results in your immediate presence.

In my work with ministers, I get them on their feet and on-camera with no notes and no pulpit. This bare and open setting lends itself to a raw and vulnerable moment. When they begin to speak, their only goal is to lose themselves in their words. At first, they are completely aware of their peers watching. And then, through the Point of Focus exercise, they become aware of the life of their words and their in-the-moment feelings. They commonly display great courage, and as they dissolve into the experience of what they are saying, the result is nothing short of miraculous - a transformation. Their blocks dissolve before our eyes, revealing the powerful, authentic self. In a recent seminar, one of the participants gasped as she watched a colleague step out from behind his blocking mechanism. It was stunning. It's not unusual to have tears of relief at having finally shed their protective devices.

Now, of the following tools for staying present, know that one or more may feel more comfortable than the others. Find a favorite.

The Task: Losing yourself in the experience
The Implementation: Make it a movie

- **Making it a movie:** Picture what you're saying, as if you're stepping into a real movie about your story in all its vivid, living color. The goal is to be *lost* in it by becoming a part of the experience and feeling of it. This works best, of course, if you're telling a story. It would be tough to see sales statistics as a movie! Try to visualize it in your head, then just fall completely into it. And, when you're immersed in the experience of it, others are immersed too. They'll be right there alongside you, experiencing it as though they had lived it. Does it take courage to let go in this way? Yes. And the reward is well worth it.

I recall one particularly profound "making it a movie" moment for Fran, our singer, when she sang for the head of a label. The stakes were high. She was very nervous in describing her hometown by practically giving a history of each century. She was out, and it wasn't going well. Thankfully the label president asked, "So what do people do for fun in your home town, count the street lights?" Fran quickly visualized her hometown as if she was back there as a teenager, standing right on the corner, and she dropped into being present and quipped, "It wasn't even that exciting. My hometown's so small, why, we don't even have street lights! We don't have lines down the middle of the road either." Here Fran actually pointed to the floor where she was seeing the street and concluded, "By the way, it's the only road we have." Fran had starred in the movie of her hometown. She had forgotten that she was talking to a label president and laughed out loud as she stepped into that experience. It took her about 10 seconds to capture him, and when she finished, they were both laughing out loud. She shared the *experience* of her hometown, not just the facts.

The Task: Wrap new words around your old
information to achieve presence
The Implementation: Use fresh words

- **Using "fresh" words:** Using the same words you have spoken before allows you to easily slip out into absence. Your brain grabs often-repeated words and can trip you up trying to find them again. Switch your words. Wrap your main themes in different words. Creating a new way of saying it will force you to be present.

We become attached to a certain sales pitch for example, because it's convenient or because we think it has the perfect words, tried and true. However, given the choice between using old words and being absent versus using new words and being present, there is little debate when you consider the value of presence.

I consistently teach this to recording artists, who are taught that "sound bites" or small snippets of the same words are the safest things to say. It's said with good intention, but it isn't true. Pre-practiced and preconceived words make it more difficult to be present because the brain tends to grab familiar words and phrases and repeat them. Much more is lost than gained because the artist is then invisible. It seems easier to the artist, I'm sure, but the outcome is not in their best interest. Also remember, if you use memorized words, or words you have to recall, you must "check out" and go to the future to find them, which means you are absent.

As we continue our exploration of the means to achieve presence, some methods are things we want to do, as in those we've discussed. But some, work by stopping things we already do. Keep in mind that with any one of these methods you can achieve presence.

Removing the "Blocking Mechanism"

Very briefly, let's connect the dots surrounding the blocking mechanisms we discussed earlier. First, the fear. We're taught to be afraid. Fear triggers self-consciousness, which creates a need for something to hide behind. That something is an act. To get into our act, we need to stay absent from what is real. It is a blocking mechanism that allows us to do that. So the act succeeds in distancing us, which makes our interactions uncomfortable and generates more fear. Plus, it confirms our earlier fear and creates massive self-consciousness which drives us to make our act better since it's our perceived protection...and that bigger and better act then disconnects us even further.

One footnote here, we do all of those interlinking steps above without any awareness. So, because there is little-to-no awareness, there is a challenge in first finding the "blocking mechanism" and then "unwiring" it from your sense of security, and finally in removing it. This is the final step in The Technology of Authentic Presence.

When I work with clients, I help them identify what their particular block is and we remove it. Once the block is removed, the act or mask falls away and they are instantly present.

Now, let's see what you can do to achieve that. First, try and get an idea of what your blocking mechanism might be. You will have one dominant block. What you're looking for is a communication pattern that you use frequently, probably when you are uncomfortable in interactions. I asked you if you could identify at least one mask or act. If you didn't identify one then, take a few minutes and do that now. Look for skills such as *voice tone* with your voice staying on a note or two; or *emphasis* with the habit of singling out no words to be emphasized; or *pacing* with your speed being medium, fast or slow, but unchanging; or *volume* with you being either all loud or all soft; or speaking *style* with long pauses between each series of three or four words. Most people are aware of a pattern that is predominant, maybe one that others have pointed out to you. Remember that these blocks show up only when you're in uncomfortable situations.

The Task: Removing the blocking mechanism
The Implementation: Stretching exercises

When you're alone and are sure you will have privacy, what I want you to do is to stretch yourself in the opposite direction from the action of your block. For example, if your block is loud volume, you will pretend that you are talking with someone who makes you nervous, someone with whom you would normally talk more loudly. I want you to say the words you would likely say to that person, but say the words very softly. It's a stretch in the opposite direction from the pull of your block. You may want to re-enact an interaction that was uncomfortable.

What that looks like:

- IF YOUR BLOCK IS *LOW VOLUME*, PRACTICE BEING REALLY LOUD, AS IN PRACTICALLY YELLING! YES, I'M SERIOUS. YOU HAVE TO STRETCH YOURSELF OUT OF THAT BLOCK. LET IT FEEL SILLY. BUT DO IT!

- IF YOUR BLOCK IS *SPEAKING FAST*, THEN SLOW DOWN, VERY SLOW.

- IF YOUR BLOCK IS *NO-EMPHASIS*, EMPHASIZE EVERY THIRD WORD AND I WANT YOU TO EXAGGERATE. YES, IT FEELS STRANGE, BUT IT'S IMPORTANT.

- IF YOU PUT A *SPACE BETWEEN EVERY WORD*, RUN YOUR WORDS TOGETHER. NO PAUSES BETWEEN WORDS AT ALL.

- IF YOU SPEAK ON *ONE OR TWO TONES*, ALLOW YOUR VOICE TO BE LYRICAL AND MOVE TWO TONES UP AND TWO TONES DOWN, ALMOST AS THOUGH YOU ARE READING A CHILDREN'S STORY WITH RELAXED VOICE INFLECTIONS.

About now, you're probably saying, "Are you serious?"

Yes, I'm serious. Remember that this kind of practice is taken as a real event by your brain apparatus and isn't perceived by the brain as a role play. It is experienced as being real, thus we can learn from role plays just as if it were happening in real life. This exercise is fully capable of ridding you of those tools that have become liabilities in your life. I know it will be uncomfortable. But honestly, you're already uncomfortable, which is why you're here. So let's do this, trusting that after your stretch, you'll come back to a natural and real medium point while losing the block and achieving the release of the act in the process. That mechanism is what has been preventing you from being present. It will be worth the stretch.

Then, in your next real interaction, you will simply focus on your words and feelings, and you'll notice that things will have shifted and that the block has just disappeared. And suddenly you will have slipped into full presence and engagement, which you will only realize when you're finished. On reflection, you will see that you were lost in the presence of that interaction.

Now, if the interaction following your stretch exercise is a particularly stressful one, give yourself a break and realize that you've set up a worst-case scenario. Go back to your exaggerated stretch work and when you're finished, make sure your next interaction is not the most pressure-packed thing you can imagine. Be kind to yourself and allow this process to work. It will happen naturally if you will allow it. Remember that you don't have a learning curve here. You already know how to be present. What is standing in your way is the blocking mechanism designed to keep you disengaged from the interaction.

Now, you've worked on your block and the techniques to help you stay present. So, if dissolving the block causes the act to fall away – you are there. Don't be surprised if you're quite powerful when you really engage. It's the power of connection.

HERE IS YOUR "PRESENCE" PLAN:

The Practice Element:

- FIRST, IDENTIFY YOUR BLOCK, THEN SPEND A FEW MINUTES SEVERAL TIMES A DAY DOING THE EXTREME OPPOSITE. YOU'LL KNOW IT'S WORKING AS YOUR BLOCK DISSOLVES.

- THEN, OVER THE NEXT SEVERAL DAYS, HAVE A DISCIPLINED INTENT TO BE PRESENT. IF YOU'RE DISTRACTED, JUST NOTICE IT AND DROP RIGHT BACK INTO BEING PRESENT. PUT NO ENERGY INTO BEING UPSET THAT YOU'RE ABSENT. NEVER FOCUS ON WHAT YOU DON'T WANT.

- CHOOSE THE TECHNIQUE FOR STAYING PRESENT THAT WORKS BEST FOR YOU:
  - ➢ POINT OF FOCUS
  - ➢ MAKE IT A MOVIE
  - ➢ FRESH WORDS

- THEN, CHART YOUR PROGRESS SO THAT YOU WILL BE AWARE OF IT. YOU MAY ALSO WANT TO CHART REACTIONS TO YOU AS THEY CHANGE. IF YOU DON'T PAY ATTENTION, IT COULD SEEM THAT THE WHOLE WORLD IS BEGINNING TO CHANGE, WHEN IN FACT, IT'S YOU WHO IS CHANGING AND THE WORLD IS SIMPLY RESPONDING TO YOU.

The Summary Element:

- YOUR FULL ATTENTION CAN BE ON ONLY ONE THING AT A TIME.
- FEAR HAS NO POWER UNLESS YOU ARE FOCUSED ON IT. REMOVE YOUR ATTENTION AND IT DISAPPEARS.
- PRESENCE AND FEAR CANNOT COEXIST.
- PRESENCE AND SELF-CONSCIOUSNESS CANNOT COEXIST
- PRESENCE AND JUDGMENT CANNOT COEXIST.
- HAVE A DISCIPLINED INTENT TO BE PRESENT.
- PRESENCE DISSOLVES THE OBSERVER, AND ALL BLOCKS AND ACTS.
- WHEN YOU INTERACT, DROP INTO EACH WORD AS YOU SAY IT, AND FEEL EACH WORD AS YOU HEAR IT. YOUR ONLY GOAL IS TO BE PRESENT.
- THE ONLY WAY TO DO IT PERFECTLY IS TO BE PERFECTLY PRESENT.
- ALWAYS PLACE YOUR FOCUS ONLY ON WHAT YOU WANT TO CREATE.

THERE IS ONLY ONE GIFT AND IT IS YOU. THERE'S ONLY ONE MEANS FOR GIVING IT AND THAT'S BY BEING *PRESENT*.

And finally, this road ends and another begins. You now have the awareness and the Technology of Authentic Presence. You also have a fresh start with a new mandate that I hope you have accepted as your own. The mandate is to let yourself matter and be of importance to the people in your life by being there in their lives, and by your willingness to be powerful through your connection with them. Those moments that you can now enter with your presence will not come your way again. Our lives are like flowing water that ripples by...allowing us to touch it...or if not, to forever miss the opportunity.

And for myself, I think the greatest gift of this journey was the day sitting in a restaurant in New York, when I realized that our fear is not about our great weakness but about our great power. Being present is the essential element in our lives because it is our connecting point. Without a connection, it doesn't matter what gift we bring to the party because we will have no way to give it. *Presence* is the means by which we give the gift that is us.

Chapter Six

The Magic of ME:
The Power of Authentic Presence

◊ We are the One gift ◊

We are led to believe that it isn't in us, that it was only in those who came before. And we're assured that we don't need it, that it isn't available, and that it's not for us to have. And we're told that we won't find it, that there's no point in searching. None of that is true. Everyday I see the gift that you bring. I see you lose your fear and hesitation to step forward and return to who you have always been. I am reminded moment by moment as I experience your courage that it is in us, and that it was never lost.

So it is with Fran, as we celebrate the close of her story and share the stories of these stunningly courageous people.

FRAN'S STORY -

What a radiant, loving woman. There's nothing about her that should be seen as anything but successful. Yes, there were heartbreaking moments when her dream was faltering. And finally it became obvious that she would have to shift gears and get on with her life, which was so hard to do. So here is the rest of Fran's story, and a hint, it involves a loving husband and two wonderful children. I'm not sure that Fran traded one dream for another. I'm not sure that's how it works. I'm guessing that she would like to have had both, but the one she got is pretty special. She's living very near her hometown. Near enough that her mom, dad and sister can spoil those children in just the right southern way. They call and visit and hug and tell stories and they spend a lot of time being happy.

And remember the authenticity lessons, the tough ones that Fran learned? The ones about being only you and all of you; and the ones about not going absent so that you can get ready to hit that high note? Well, she got it, and although she did not get the recording deal, she got something more important. Fran got Fran back.

So if anyone in the southern part of this country needs a very wise and talented vocal coach, you should look her up. Fran teaches so much more than just singing.

YOUR AUTHENTIC PRESENCE
IS THE GREATEST GIFT OF ALL.

MARY'S STORY -

"Mary," a graduate nursing student was asked to briefly introduce a classmate during a small group exercise. The class of 25 students was seated and each was doing the same exercise. When it was Mary's turn and all eyes focused on her, she immediately lowered her head, broke into tears, jumped up and ran out of the room. When the professor questioned her later, Mary said, "I can't talk with anyone watching me." Her professor was surprised, as Mary was working on a Master's Degree in a helping profession – one that required extensive face-to-face communication with patients, families and medical staff. This particular course, which focused on "change strategies," required that each student stand in front of the class and do a 10-minute presentation of a personal change project on which they were currently working. When her professor asked Mary about being able to do her presentation she responded, "You'll just have to fail me. I can't do it." The professor reminded Mary that this course was a requirement for completing her Master's Degree. Mary stated emphatically that she would just have to fail.

At that point, Mary was referred for M.E. coaching. After six hours of intensive presence work, she was ready. And on the last day of class, to her professor's astonishment, Mary stood up and slowly walked to the front of the room. She looked her classmates in the eye and over the next 10 minutes she confidently, professionally and passionately presented her personal change project which she entitled, "Overcoming the Fear of Being Watched by Others." Mary made an "A" and graduated from the program. Her professor said, "It was a magical transformation that I wasn't sure was possible." Today, Mary is a successful nurse practitioner.

THE POWER OF FULL PRESENCE
IS A PRACTICAL REALITY,
REMOVING A LIFETIME OF OBSTACLES.

SAM'S STORY -

"Sam" was an experienced salesperson who just thought he would like to be better. I don't think he expected to learn anything of significance. As corporate people like to say, "If I just get one new idea, my time will have been well spent." So after a few sessions and a lot of work with implementing the power of presence into his sales persuasion, Sam was to make a sales call the following day. He was calling on a top executive he didn't know and was asking for business in an industry that had been hard hit by a tough economy. Sam's appointment was at 2. At 2:30, my phone rang. It was Sam. He said, "It was like he knew I was coming. I know you didn't call him. Did you? No, of course not. And not only that, but it was like he knew what I was going to ask for. And not only that, it seemed like he had decided to give me what I asked for before I ever got there. It was too easy. But that's not the only thing. Last night I got a phone call from a guy I would normally not talk to. He had stopped talking to me a few years back when I became successful in my business. He was jealous, and recently he has wanted to be friends again. But I hadn't been able to talk to him because I've been so angry. So last night when the phone rang, I decided that I would try being present and see if I could hold my temper. He started talking, and the next time I looked at the clock we had been talking for 20 minutes, and the best part is that I totally forgot that I was mad. I even forgot that I was trying to be present. I just let it happen. We talked. I don't know if we'll be best friends, or even friends at all. But he apologized and choked up a little, and I felt something. I really did. He's a good guy. I had forgotten."

The power of removing fear from the equation when two people are sitting together can't be overstated. That's what Sam experienced. Most sales people are afraid to let up on the pressure. That's why most sales people create the objections that they then have to overcome.

BEING PRESENT IS THE MOST NATURAL THING
WE KNOW.
IT IS HOW WE ARE FED AND LED;
AND ANYTHING THAT IS ITS OPPOSITE
IS A "NO-THING" THAT CAN BE DISSOLVED
IN THAT PRESENT MOMENT.

GARY'S STORY –

A preacher delivered a very telling story to the group. "Gary" had joked throughout the seminar about literally everything. He was driven to lighten up every moment, even just after someone tearfully described losing a loved one. This minister couldn't sit still when the subject went deep. And then a fascinating thing happened.

He was smiling and grinning his way through the story of a car wreck he had experienced. He was the only person in the room smiling as he told of driving at night, from the city into a little country town where he rolled his car down an embankment and lost consciousness. Remember that his delivery was very light. Here are the words he spoke: "I remember waking up in the back of what seemed to be a dark ambulance. I couldn't seem to move, and all I could hear was the sound of the road rushing by as the ambulance sped along. I was facing the back window and suddenly a street light flashed across it and I saw the words 'Funeral Home.' Well, I just didn't know what to think or do. Here I was in a hearse. I guess I couldn't understand how I could be awake and reading those words. It was somewhat funny. And it turned out that the hearse from the funeral home doubled as the town's ambulance." That was his story. Everyone in the room was quiet and somber as they watched him do a complete mismatch between what he said and how he said it. He was clearly blocking all deep feelings about everything so that he could evade reliving that one traumatic experience.

It was not an accident that he had chosen that particular story. And so I knew that while he was still afraid, he seemed to be giving himself permission to step into this experience and be present. So, I asked him if he would do it again and start at the moment he awoke inside that vehicle. And I asked him not to tell the story in a way that he had ever told it before. "You have one goal," I told him. "I want you to see and feel that moment when you woke up, and tell us about it. If I sense that you aren't back there inside that vehicle, I will remind you. Otherwise I won't say a word." He tried to start by throwing a funny line. And so we gently restarted each time he blocked going there. We did this several times until he mustered his courage. Finally, he was inside. And he said, "I woke up and when I saw those words on the back window I felt a cold shiver and I wanted to scream because I knew I was dead." And he cried. It was something he had run from for years and now he wouldn't let himself run anymore. He moved to the floor, sat down and sobbed. Tears ran down his face and in halting speech, he described the agony he felt as he thought that hearse was taking his body to the funeral home. He cried about his life and all the things he had done and those things he could now never undo. And he agonized about the things that had gone unspoken, knowing that they could now never be said. He cried until there were no more tears and there was no more sound. His body sat still and his eyes stared at the floor. It was one of those moments when we all wanted to help, but we knew better. So there was silence until he got up and sat back in his chair. He was exhausted and so were we all. As we took a break, I noticed a line forming of those who wanted to express their thanks to him for what he had courageously done and for the gift it had been to them. "An inspiration," they said.

What I find amazing about Gary is his level of courage. First, he chose that story. He didn't have to. Then he blocked his feelings and stayed absent the way he consistently operated, knowing that he would get called on it. And after that, for him to gather the courage to do what he had so feared and to face that moment he had dreaded. Such courage.

One final point about Gary and about all of you. Every one of you has an innate integrity that is perfect. You may or may not be aware of it, but I've seen it thousands of times. It is there and it surfaces in those "hero" moments, like this one for Gary.

DO YOU LOSE YOURSELF,

BY GIVING YOURSELF?

DO YOU SAVE YOURSELF,

BY HIDING YOURSELF?

"Corinne" had stuttered since the day she began talking. She was one of two sisters living in Haiti. When Corinne stumbled over her early words, her 5-year old sister began to actually speak for her. Corinne would try to talk and her sister would put the sounds into understandable words. She was always by Corinne's side throughout her childhood, being her voice.

Then the day came for Corinne to move to America and study healthcare at a prestigious university. She was very bright, made excellent grades in her home country and was now facing life without her "interpreter." And so, fighting through the fear, she made the move and began graduate school. She stuttered with every sound, and each word was jumbled. She worked hard at her studies, kept to herself, stayed disengaged from social activities, seldom spoke a word outside of class, and made it into her advanced studies. It was then that she was advised to seek help with her speech. Corinne had heard about M.E. coaching and asked for a meeting. After I had spoken with her by phone and agreed to see her, I wasn't at all sure that this technology was what she needed. This would be the first time a stutterer had asked for help through M.E. coaching.

The day Corinne arrived and we sat down, I told her that I knew very little of the complex issue with which she was dealing. Corinne began to tell her story, and it was when I heard her say these words, "I try not to open my mouth because I know if I speak I will stutter. I sit there and worry about it because I know the first sound out of my mouth will be a stutter which no one can understand." Then I knew. Corinne might be in the right place after all. I realized that her attention was moving out into the future being fearful of her stuttering, and that being present could possibly be the solution. We worked about eight hours with the goal of her holding onto being present regardless of what she feared was looming in the future. That future, for Corinne, was a lifetime of pain, boiled down to a focus on one moment, the moment just ahead. And all her fear was waiting there.

After the first session, she had the concept and was embarrassed that she couldn't yet put it into action. After the second session, she spent half the time not remembering her habit of being afraid before she spoke. She was now forgetting to go into the future and be afraid. She would start a sentence perfectly and only when she remembered and focused on her fear did she begin to stutter.

By the end of session four, Corinne had stopped stuttering most of the time. She later told me of the first time she had said, "hello" to another student as they walked across campus. And she told me she had called her sister and was so proud to have gotten through that conversation in which her sister heard her speak clearly for the first time in their lives.

At Corinne's graduation, her sister went on stage to be with her as she accepted her diploma. No translator needed.

> PRESENCE IS THE LIGHT WITHIN EACH OF US...
> ILLUMINATING AND CONNECTING US ALL. .
> IT CAN BE TRUSTED AS A POWERFUL GIFT.

RANDY'S STORY -

I was working with a first line supervisor at a manufacturing plant and we were making strides on what I was calling "People Building." It was a new form of interaction skills containing a module about focus and attention during conflict. I coached each supervisor in four or five different scenarios in which they dealt with a tough problem across the desk from their employee. They each learned the importance of focus and attention especially when there was conflict. I later learned that Randy, one of the supervisors, was having a problem with his ninth-grade son failing school. And what was beginning to happen, which I wouldn't learn until later, was that Randy was practicing what he was learning at work on his son. Now realize that Randy didn't know what to do about his son's grades and also that his son didn't want Randy's help. But listen to what Randy began doing every night when he got home. While the family was getting ready for dinner, Randy would listen to what little his son would say. Now the rule in my coaching was that you're cheating if you aren't focused, engaged and listening. It's not necessary to talk, in fact it's often better if you don't. But you must engage and listen. So that's what Randy was doing at home. He listened for ten minutes here and there every night. As the weeks went by, Randy did nothing different, but his son did. His boy began to stretch the 10 minutes setting the table with his dad to 20 minutes, talking to his father all the while. Then after dinner, Randy found his son having more questions...about homework, about friendships, about girl friends... about almost anything. Randy just chalked it up to his son having some "Dad questions" since he was a young teenager.

Time passed and the same pattern continued. Then one day Randy's son brought home his report card to be signed. His grades had gotten better. That improvement continued over the next three years and the day for graduation arrived. The 18-year old graduating senior stood in cap and gown on the high school stage with the principal proudly announcing that Randy's son had been accepted at The Air Force Academy. Randy had tears in his eyes when he told me the story. And he said, "I don't know exactly what happened, except that I started hearing him when I listened to him. I met my son. And it changed both our lives. I will never be the same."

Randy had been unintentionally disconnected from his son. And they both paid the price. Something had been missing and Randy finally realized it had been him.

TO BE PRESENT IS TO BE FEARLESS,

WHICH IS TO BE FREE...

THERE IS MORE TO FREEDOM

THAN ANY OF US KNOW...

BECAUSE WE HAVE NOT SEEN IT

ENOUGH TO KNOW IT...

THERE IS ONE BARRIER ALONE,

AND IT IS NOW WITHIN OUR CONTROL...

BUT WE HAVE TO CHOOSE...

WILL IT BE THE CHOICE TO LOOK FEAR IN THE FACE

AND BE TRAPPED WITHIN IT FOREVER?

OR WILL IT BE THE MORE DIFFICULT,

MORE COURAGEOUS CHOICE TO BE

PRESENT WITHIN EVERY MOMENT,

COMPLETE WITH ITS EVERY THOUGHT

AND FEELING?

THE FORMER IS TO BE ENSLAVED...

THE LATTER IS A PURE AND SIMPLE FREEDOM.

....And so the Gift is given and the children dance unafraid, twirling endlessly in the pure joy of Being.

And their Lightness beckons others to follow...

...and so it is.

And if we may leave you with this wish and our great hope that you will, after this day, never again be what is missing in your life.

Jeri & Cole

We invite you to share your story

and access downloads on M.E. Technology

www.MyMissingElement.com

References

1. *Oxford American Dictionary*. New York: Avon Books; 1980.

2. Kim YJ, Grabowecky M, Paller KA, Muthu K, Suzuki S. Attention induces synchronization-based response gain in steady-state visual evoked potentials. *Nature Neuroscience*. 2007;10 (11).

3. Kim YJ, Grabowecky M, Paller KA, Muthu K, Suzuki S. Paying attention sets off symphony of cell synchronization. *Science Daily*. 2006.

4. Mack A, Rock I. Inattentional blindness. In: Wright RD, ed. *Visual Attention.* New York: Oxford Press; 1998:61.

5. Simons DJ, Chabris CF. Gorillas in Our Midst: Sustained Inattentional Blindness for Dynamic Events. *Perception.* 1999;28 (9):1059-74. Available from: Pubmed – Indexed for MEDLINE. Accessed April 28, 2009.

6. Ehninger D, Gronbeck B, McKerrow A, Monroe A. *Principles and Types of Speech Communication. 10th ed.* Glenville: Scott Foresman and Company; 1986.

7. Mehrabian A, Weiner M. Decoding of inconsistent communications. *Journal of Personality and Social Psychology.* 1967; 6:109-114.

8. Cherry EC. Some experiments on the recognition of speech, with one and two ears. *Journal of the Acoustical Society of America.* 1953; 25:975-979.

9. Wright R. *Visual Attention: Vancouver Studies In Cognitive Science,* Vol 8. New York: Oxford University Press; 1998.

24468579R00129

Made in the USA
Lexington, KY
20 July 2013